FORTIFIED BY AI

A Security Leader's Guide to Governance, Defense, and the Operating Model That Holds

PARVESH AHLAWAT

notionpress.com

INDIA • SINGAPORE • MALAYSIA

ISBN
Paperback 979-8-90319-340-0
Hardcase 979-8-90479-912-0

CONTENTS

Acknowledgments 13

Preface 15

- **Why I Wrote This Book** 16
- **What This Book Covers** 16
- **Who This Book Is For** 17
- **A Note from the Author** 18

PART 1 FOUNDATIONS (BASICS OF AI & CYBERSECURITY) 19

1. Why AI Is Transforming Cybersecurity 21

- The "Scale vs. Speed" Breaking Point 21
- Reality Check: The Forces Shaping Modern Cybersecurity 22
- Key Data Points and Supporting Evidence 24
- Insights and Practical Frameworks 24
  - *The Expanded Threat Landscape: Different Surfaces, One Program* 24
  - *AI as a Force Multiplier Across the Security Stack* 25
  - *The Secure SDLC, End to End: Build, Deploy, Run, Observe* 26
  - *Runtime Sensors and Why Context Wins* 28
  - *Human-in-the-Loop, Human-on-the-Loop, Human-out* 29
  - *Business Impact and ROI: Metrics Leaders Can Defend* 29
  - *Inevitable Adoption, and Why Discipline Is the Differentiator* 30
- Case Studies 31
  - *Case Study 1: GenAI Phishing and Deepfake Surge* 31
  - *Case Study 2: Shadow AI and the Source Code That Went Public* 31
  - *Case Study 3: Cross-Surface Correlation Catches a Quiet Intrusion* 32

Regulations and Standards: A Global View 32

KPIs to Track 33

Risks and Guardrails 34

Executive Takeaways 36

End-of-Chapter Reflection Questions 37

2. Artificial Intelligence Basics for Security Professionals 39

The Day "AI" Stopped Being a Buzzword 39

A Working Taxonomy: Where Each Term Fits 40

Key Properties Leaders should Internalize 41

Insights and Practical Frameworks 41

Machine Learning 101 41

Supervised vs Unsupervised: Known Threats vs Unknown Threats 41

Deep Learning: Power, Opacity, Trade-offs 42

NLP and Language Models in Security 42

Generative AI and Foundation Models 43

Public vs Private Models: Deployment Choices 43

AI Agents and Agentic AI: What Changes When AI Acts 44

MCP: How Agents Connect to the Real World 44

Data as Fuel, and What It Demands 46

Limits and Misconceptions 46

OWASP Top 10 for LLM Applications: Reference Card 47

AI Red-Teaming: Testing Before Attackers Do 48

Case Studies 49

Case Study 1: A Machine Learning Malware Classifier 49

Case Study 2: Unsupervised Login Anomaly Detection 49

KPIs to Track 50

Risks and Guardrails 51

Executive Takeaways 51

End-of-Chapter Reflection Questions 52

3. Cybersecurity Fundamentals—Threats, Risks, and the CIA Triad **53**

You Can't "AI" Your Way Around Fundamentals 53

Fundamentals First: A Shared Language 54

Key Data Points and Supporting Evidence 54

Insights and Practical Frameworks 55

The CIA Triad, Extended 55

Beyond CIA: AAA, Zero Trust, Defense in Depth 56

The Expanded Attack Vector Landscape 57

Risk = Likelihood × Impact, and Practical Risk Frameworks 59

Why the Baseline Still Decides Outcomes 60

Mapping a Ransomware Attack Across the CIA Triad 61

Attack Vectors vs AI-Enhanced Defenses 61

Case Study: NotPetya, Maersk, and the Cost of Weak Fundamentals 63

KPIs to Track 64

Risks and Guardrails 65

Executive Takeaways 66

End-of-Chapter Reflection Questions 67

PART 2 AI IN ACTION (PRACTICAL SECURITY APPLICATIONS) **69**

4. AI-Powered Secure Software Development Lifecycle **71**

The Speed Gap That Broke Traditional SSDLC 71

The Modern Development Reality 72

Key Data Points and Supporting Evidence 73

Insights and Practical Frameworks 73

The AI-Enhanced SSDLC: A Closer Look 73

Secure-by-Design with AI: Continuous Threat Modeling 74

Agentic AI in the Development Phase 75

AI-Driven CI/CD Pipeline Security 76

AI-Enhanced Security Testing 78

AI-Led Remediation and Validation 79

Build-Deploy-Run: Closing the Lifecycle 80

Case Studies 81

Case Study 1: Agentic Dev Adoption at a FinTech 81

Case Study 2: Preventing a CI/CD Supply-Chain Compromise 82

KPIs to Track 83

Risks and Guardrails 84

Executive Takeaways 85

End-of-Chapter Reflection Questions 86

5. AI-Powered Security Operations Center 87

When Every Minute Starts Costing You 87

From Traditional SOC to AI-SOC 88

Key Data Points and Supporting Evidence 88

Insights and Practical Frameworks 89

AI-Driven Threat Detection and Prevention 89

Agentic AI for SOC Operations 90

AI-Assisted Incident Response 91

AI-Powered Forensics and Root Cause Analysis 92

The Closed Loop: SSDLC ↔ SOC 92

The Realistic Trajectory: Where AI-SOC Is Heading 93

IR Before vs After AI: A Comparison 94

Case Studies 94

Case Study 1: AI-Augmented SOC at DEF Logistics 94

Case Study 2: Automated Incident Response at XYZ Bank 95

Case Study 3: Cross-Surface Forensics After a Supply-Chain Incident 96

KPIs to Track 97

Risks and Guardrails 98

Executive Takeaways 99

End-of-Chapter Reflection Questions 100

6. Identity, Data, SaaS, and AI Security—The Adaptive Control Plane 101

Four Surfaces, One Operating Model 101

Identity Security: How AI Helps 101

Data Security: How AI Helps 102

SaaS Security: How AI Helps 103

AI Security: How AI Helps Secure AI 104

How AI Helps: A Cross-Domain View 105

Case Study: Adaptive Authentication and SaaS Governance at SecureBank 106

KPIs to Track 106

Risks and Guardrails 107

Executive Takeaways 108

End-of-Chapter Reflection Questions 108

PART 3 ADVANCED TOPICS & GOVERNANCE 111

7. Adversarial AI and Emerging Risks 113

When Defenders Use AI, Attackers Learn Faster Too 113

The Three Layers of Adversarial AI Risk 113

Insights and Practical Frameworks 114

Evasion: How Attackers Slip Past AI Defenses 114

Poisoning: Corrupting What the Model Learns 115

Model Theft, Extraction, and Privacy Attacks 115

Prompt Injection and Agent Manipulation 116

Deepfakes and Synthetic Identity: Attacking Human Trust 117

Autonomous Offensive Agents: The Forward Trajectory 117

Defend the AI Lifecycle: A Working Model 118

Adversarial Tactics and Practical Defenses 118
Case Studies 119
Case Study 1: Attackers Adapting to an AI Email Filter *119*
Case Study 2: Adversarial Evasion Against a Malware Classifier *120*
KPIs to Track 120
Risks and Guardrails 121
Executive Takeaways 122
End-of-Chapter Reflection Questions 123

8. Ethics, Privacy, and Regulatory Compliance **125**
Trust Turns into a Security Control 125
The Regulatory and Framework Landscape 125
ISO/IEC 42001: The AI Management System in Practice 127
Sub-Processor Due Diligence: Onboarding AI Tools and SaaS 128
What to Evaluate Before Onboarding *128*
GRC Agents: Continuous Compliance From Live Evidence 129
Ethics, Fairness, and Human Oversight 130
Data Minimization with Security Intent *130*
Fairness, Bias, and Disparity as Quality Control *131*
Human Oversight and Contestability *131*
Structured Decision Logging: The Audit Trail That Works *131*
Case Study: Employee Monitoring AI Under GDPR and DPDPA Pressure 132
KPIs to Track 133
Risks and Guardrails 133
Executive Takeaways 134
End-of-Chapter Reflection Questions 135

9. The Road Ahead—Quantum, Sovereign AI, and the Evolving Security Landscape 137
The Next Few Years Will Feel Faster and Wider 137
Quantum Readiness and Post-Quantum Migration 137
Crypto Agility as the Practical Starting Point *138*
Case Study: Crypto Inventory at a Global Bank *138*
Sovereign AI and Data Sovereignty 139
Edge AI and Cyber-Physical Convergence 140
AI and the Future of Security Talent 140
Planning Anchors: What to Start, Watch, and Invest In 141
KPIs to Track 142
Risks and Guardrails 143
Executive Takeaways 143
End-of-Chapter Reflection Questions 144

10. The 6-System Operating Model—From Pilot to Scale 145
Why Pilots Fade and Programs Stall 145
The Six Systems 145
System 1: Outcomes and Scope *145*
System 2: Data Readiness and Integration *146*
System 3: Phased Deployment *146*
System 4: Measurable Performance *146*
System 5: Governance and Guardrails *146*
System 6: Continuous Improvement *147*
Readiness Assessment: Where Are You Today? 147
A 12-Month Plan Leaders Can Run 148
The Executive Dashboard That Fits on One Screen 149
Two Sprints to Value in 30 Days 149
Case Study: From Pilot to Policy in 90 Days 149

Executive Takeaways 150

End-of-Chapter Reflection Questions 151

Conclusion Security With AI That Holds Up in Real Conditions 153

What Holds Up 153

The Path from Interest to Capability 154

A Final Thought 154

Annexures AI-Driven Security in Practice 155

Annexure A AI-Driven Cloud Defense in Practice 157

Bridging Strategy and Execution in Modern Cloud Security 157

1. From AI Strategy to Cloud Reality 157

2. Understanding the Upwind CNAPP Architecture 157

3. AI Embedded in the Upwind Platform: Beyond Marketing Claims 158

4. Defending Against Cloud Configuration Risks with Runtime Context 158

5. Runtime Sensors for Vulnerability and Threat Detection 158

6. AI Security and Agentic Workloads 159

7. Continuous Improvement of Cloud Security Posture 159

8. Strategic Fit for Security Leaders 159

9. Learn More and Engage 160

Closing Perspective 160

Annexure B AI-Driven Offensive Security in Practice 161

Bridging Strategy and Execution in Modern Application Security 161

1. From AI Strategy to Offensive Security Reality 161

2. Understanding the Astra Security Platform Architecture 161

3. AI Embedded in Astra: Beyond Automation 162

4. AI-Assisted Pentesting and Red-Team-Style Thinking 162

5. Trust Platform and Verifiable Security Posture 163

6. CREST-Aligned and Expert-Led Testing 163

7. Continuous Improvement of Application Security Posture *163*

8. Strategic Fit for Security Leaders *164*

Closing Perspective *164*

Annexure C AI-Driven Application Security Posture Management in Practice **165**

Bridging Strategy and Execution in Modern Application Security Posture *165*

1. From AI Strategy to Application Security Posture Reality *165*

2. Understanding the OX Security Platform Architecture *166*

3. AI Embedded in OX Security: Beyond Aggregation *166*

4. Securing the Software Supply Chain with PBOM and OSC&R *167*

5. AI-Assisted Remediation and Developer Collaboration *167*

6. VibeSec™: Active Runtime Protection *167*

7. Compliance and Regulatory Alignment *168*

8. Strategic Fit for Security Leaders *168*

9. Learn More and Engage *169*

Closing Perspective *169*

About the Author **171**

Why This Book Exists **172**

ACKNOWLEDGMENTS

A book like this does not happen in isolation. It draws from thousands of conversations, countless late nights, and the quiet support of people who believed in the work even when progress felt slow.

My deepest gratitude goes to my family. To my wife, who has stood by my side through every career transition, every late-night incident call, every weekend spent writing instead of being present. She never once asked me to stop. She asked how it was going, whether I had eaten, and whether the chapter was turning out the way I wanted. That kind of patience is not small. It is the foundation that made this book possible. To my son, who watched his father spend evenings at a keyboard and weekends lost in drafts, and who still greeted every morning with the kind of energy that reminded me why the work matters. You both gave me the space to do this, and I will never take that for granted.

To my late father—this one is harder to write.

He is not here to hold this book. He will not see his name on this page. And yet, he is in every page of it. He was a man of simple conviction and extraordinary faith in education. He did not know cybersecurity. He did not know about AI. But he knew something more fundamental: that learning is the one thing nobody can take away from you, and that it compounds in ways you cannot predict when you begin.

When things were difficult—and in a long career, they sometimes were—I heard his voice. The same words, every time. Clear, steady, without drama:

"Beta, kuch bhi ho jaye, padhte rahna."

"Son, whatever happens, keep on learning."

That line carried me through exams, through military training, through career changes, through incidents that felt overwhelming, and through the doubt that comes with writing a book about a field that changes faster than anyone can fully keep up with. He gave me the most durable instruction I have ever received. I wish I could hand him a copy and watch him turn the pages, even though he would not have understood most of the words. He would have understood that his son kept learning. That would have been enough for him. It is enough for me.

Papa, this book is for you.

Mentors Who Shaped the Journey: No career of consequence is built alone. I have been fortunate to serve under and learn from leaders who saw potential before I saw it in myself, who demanded excellence without demanding conformity, and who taught by example that leadership is service.

Air Cmde RN Gaekwad (Retd), whose clarity of thought and operational rigor set the standard I have tried to carry into every role since. Group Captain Prince Devaraj (Retd), who showed me that technical depth and strategic vision are not opposing forces but complementary ones.

And Benjamin Cercone, whose mentorship in the technology industry helped me see cybersecurity not as a technical function but as a business discipline—one that earns its place by making the organization stronger, not by making itself louder. His influence shaped how I think about security leadership, security program design, and the art of building trust with stakeholders who do not speak security's language.

To each of you: thank you. The lessons you taught are woven into this book, even where your names do not appear.

To Every Colleague: To every security engineer & SOC analyst who taught me what alert fatigue actually feels like at 3 AM. To every developer who showed me why security gates need to be fast to be used. To every legal and GRC professional who helped me understand that governance is not overhead but protection. To every executive who asked the hard questions that forced clarity. To every team I have had the privilege of leading—your work, your resilience, your willingness to learn and adapt under pressure, is what this book is about.

This book is for the practitioner community. If it helps one team make a better decision during a difficult moment, it has earned its place.

– Parvesh Ahlawat

PREFACE

The call came on a Tuesday evening. I was driving home from the office, thinking about dinner, when my phone lit up with a message from our SOC lead. A routine alert had turned into something that did not look routine at all. By the time I reached home, I was on a bridge call with six people across three time zones, and dinner was forgotten. We spent the next fourteen hours piecing together what happened—tracing a phishing email through a compromised credential, into a cloud workload, across a SaaS integration nobody on the security team had sanctioned, and toward a data store that held customer records we were contractually obligated to protect.

We contained it. Nobody lost data. The customer never knew. But that night, something changed in how I thought about the work.

I had spent over two decades in cybersecurity by then—building application security programs, standing up cloud security postures, running security operations, advising boards and CXOs on risk and resilience. I had seen enough incidents to know that the technical part is rarely the hardest part. The hardest part is the gap between what the team knows it should do and what the team can actually do at the speed the situation demands. That gap is where incidents become breaches, where containment becomes crisis management, and where the difference between a prepared organization and an unprepared one becomes painfully visible.

AI had been showing up in our tools for a few years by then—in detection engines, in email filters, in identity analytics. But that night, watching the correlation engine link a phishing email, an identity anomaly, a cloud access pattern, and a SaaS data flow into a single coherent narrative in seconds—work that would have taken our team hours of manual log pivoting—I saw something shift. AI was not a feature in a vendor deck anymore. It was the reason we contained the incident before the attacker completed the exfiltration. It was also the reason we discovered a SaaS integration our controls had never covered, because the same AI that helped us respond also exposed a governance gap we had not measured.

That duality—AI as both the capability that saves you and the surface that exposes you—is what this book is about.

Why I Wrote This Book

I wrote this book because I could not find the book I needed. There were plenty of books about AI—what it is, how it works, and why it matters. There were plenty of books about cybersecurity—frameworks, architectures, and incident responses. But there were very few that sat at the intersection where I spend my working life: the place where a security leader has to decide whether to trust an AI recommendation to isolate a production system at 3 AM, whether to let an agentic coding tool access the internal repository, whether to deploy adaptive authentication that treats a login from Mumbai differently from a login from a geography the model has never seen, and whether the governance around all of it will hold up when a regulator asks to see the evidence.

The questions I faced daily were not theoretical. They were operational. Which AI systems influence our security decisions, and who owns each one? What happens when the model drifts, and nobody notices? How do I explain to the board that we need AI to keep up with attackers, while also explaining that the AI itself needs securing? How do I adopt agentic development tools without leaking source code through a SaaS ecosystem our legal team has never reviewed? How do I comply with the Digital Personal Data Protection Act (DPDPA) in India, GDPR in Europe, the EU AI Act, and other global and local regulations (such as CPRA/CCPA in the US, UK GDPR, Brazil's LGPD, China's PIPL, Singapore's PDPA, and emerging AI governance frameworks), all at the same time, with the same team, without drowning in paperwork?

I looked for a book that answered these questions practically—with frameworks I could use, examples I could recognize, and a tone that respected the reality of the work without drowning in hype or academic distance. I did not find it. So, I decided to write it.

What This Book Covers

The book is structured as a journey from foundations to operations to governance to future readiness.

Part I lays the groundwork. Chapter 1 frames why AI has become central to cybersecurity and introduces the six surfaces—code, cloud, data, identity, endpoint, and OT, and AI itself—that organize the rest of the book. Chapter 2 gives security professionals the AI vocabulary they need—machine learning, deep learning, generative AI, agents, agentic AI, MCP, the OWASP Top 10 for LLM, and AI red-teaming—without requiring a data-science background. Chapter 3 revisits cybersecurity fundamentals through an expanded lens: the CIA triad extended with privacy and authenticity, zero trust, defense in depth, and the full modern attack-vector landscape.

Part II puts AI into action across the two halves of modern security operations. Chapter 4 covers the AI-powered Secure SDLC—from threat modeling and agentic development through CI/CD pipeline security, AI-enhanced testing, auto-remediation with human-in-the-loop tiering, and the critical bridge into runtime. Chapter 5 covers the AI-powered SOC—cross-surface detection, agentic investigation, automated response with tiered oversight, AI-driven forensics, and the closed loop where SOC findings flow back into the SSDLC to prevent the next incident. Chapter 6 treats identity, data, SaaS, and AI security as a unified adaptive control plane, showing how AI helps across all four surfaces.

Part III addresses the advanced topics and governance that determine whether AI security programs earn trust and survive scrutiny. Chapter 7 maps adversarial AI risk across three layers—attackers weaponizing AI, evading AI defenses, and targeting AI systems directly. Chapter 8 covers ethics, privacy, and regulatory compliance as a GRC practitioner would: every major framework, ISO 42001 in practice, sub-processor due diligence, geolocation requirements, and GRC agents that pull evidence from live systems continuously. Chapter 9 looks ahead—quantum readiness, sovereign AI, edge and cyber-physical convergence, and the evolution of security talent in an AI-augmented world. Chapter 10 provides the operating model that holds it all together: the six-system framework, a readiness assessment matrix, a twelve-month plan, an executive dashboard, and a thirty-day sprint to first value.

You can read this book straight through, since the structure builds a consistent way of thinking. Or you can read it based on immediate priorities. Leaders can start with Chapters 1 and 10 for the strategic frame and operating model, then go deeper into the domains that matter most. Practitioners can start with Chapters 4 and 5 for the build-and-run reality, then work outward into identity, adversarial risk, and governance. Either path works because every chapter cross-references the others, and the core themes—fundamentals first, human-in-the-loop discipline, the closed feedback loop, governance as daily work—run consistently from the first page to the last.

Who This Book Is For

This book is written for security leaders who want results rather than slogans. For CISOs and security directors who need to explain AI adoption to a board in business terms and then go back to the SOC and make it work in production. For engineers and analysts who must configure, tune, and trust AI-driven tools in real environments where false positives erode confidence and false negatives create incidents. For architects and developers who need to understand what secure-by-design means when the development tool itself is an AI agent with access to the codebase. For GRC professionals who need to map AI systems to ISO 42001, DPDPA, GDPR, and the EU AI

Act without losing their minds. And for executives who need a clear way to evaluate risk, measure progress, and hold their teams accountable without getting pulled into marketing language.

If you work in security and AI is part of your reality—whether you chose it or it was chosen for you—this book is for you.

A Note from the Author

This book represents my best understanding of a field that is evolving faster than any single person can fully keep up with. AI in cybersecurity is not a settled discipline. New techniques emerge, new attack patterns surface, new regulations take effect, and new tools reshape workflows—sometimes within the span of a single quarter. I have done my best to ground every claim in operational experience, published research, and established frameworks, and to distinguish clearly between what is proven and what is emerging. That said, this book may contain errors. Some details may have shifted between the time of writing and the time of reading. Some opinions may be overtaken by new evidence. I am learning alongside you, and I believe that is the right posture for anyone working at the intersection of AI and security today. If you find something that could be better, I welcome the conversation. The goal has always been to be useful, not to be perfect. Security is practice, not a destination. So is writing about it.

Part 1

FOUNDATIONS (BASICS OF AI & CYBERSECURITY)

Chapter 1

WHY AI IS TRANSFORMING CYBERSECURITY

The "Scale vs. Speed" Breaking Point

Security leaders have long framed cyber risk as a race. Adversaries scale operations; defenders push for speed in detection, decision-making, and containment. Over the last few years, many teams have watched that race reach a breaking point. Attacker capability has compounded quickly. Defender workflows, for the most part, still rely on humans stitching together evidence across several tools, ticket queues, and approval chains, and that gap now shows up in every corner of the business, not only the inbox.

Generative AI tools produce phishing and business email compromise messages with clean language and relevant context, and the same systems generate endless variants quickly enough that static indicators age fast. Deepfake voice and video reinforce these attempts, especially during workflows that depend on urgency and authority—vendor payment changes, executive approvals, payroll queries, procurement exceptions, customer refunds. A single message can represent a current initiative, mirror the tone of an executive, and land at the exact moment people feel pressure to respond quickly, which turns ordinary work into a high-risk decision point.

That pressure is real, and it is only one slice of what we have been seeing. Intrusions progress quickly without loud malware signals, because credential theft, session hijacking, and token abuse allow attackers to move through identity systems and cloud consoles with fewer obvious flags. Many incidents begin with a message, move into identity misuse, and spread into SaaS and cloud workloads, with each step leaving traces in a different system. Analysts often spend hours assembling fragments—email artifacts, mailbox rule changes, authentication logs, endpoint trails, cloud access events—while attackers use the same window to find privileged access, locate valuable data, and stage exfiltration.

Meanwhile, the surface itself has grown. Developers write code with AI assistants. Data scientists spin up notebooks connected to production data. Operations teams adopt SaaS platforms that clone source repositories into third-party ecosystems. Factory floors and logistics fleets add edge devices that never see a traditional SOC playbook. Ransomware ecosystems have continued to evolve through fragmentation and rebranding, while data-theft-plus-extortion patterns have expanded. The old center of gravity—email and endpoint—is still important, but it is no longer the whole map.

This is where security AI and automation become central to the operating model. Recent industry reporting consistently links extensive use of security AI and automation with shorter breach lifecycles and lower breach costs, because earlier detection and faster containment reduce downtime, reduce recovery effort, and limit how far an adversary can spread once a foothold exists. The leadership goal becomes straightforward: restore defender speed against attacker scale while keeping decisions accountable and systems governed.

Reality Check: The Forces Shaping Modern Cybersecurity

Five forces shape the environment most security programs operate in today.

Attackers move at machine speed across every surface. Social engineering accelerated sharply once generative models became commodity infrastructure. Attacks now arrive with polished language, strong personalization, and frequent reinforcement through synthetic voice or video. The same acceleration appears in code-level attacks, cloud reconnaissance, and identity abuse. Clues that used to help—awkward phrasing, mismatched tone, noisy scanning—provide less signal, which places greater weight on context, identity patterns, and cross-domain correlation.

Shadow AI has quietly moved inside the perimeter. Employees paste sensitive data into public chat assistants to summarize contracts, debug code, or draft customer responses. Teams stand up unsanctioned AI tools because approved options feel slow. We have seen, repeatedly, enterprises where ten to twenty percent of employees use AI services their security team has no visibility into, and where regulated data—customer records, financial forecasts, unreleased product details—ends up in prompts crossing organizational boundaries. The risk is rarely one dramatic leak; it is a steady drip that an inventory cannot see, and a DLP rule cannot catch without deliberate control.

Author's note–Shadow AI in practice

A financial services firm found, through outbound traffic analysis, that roughly sixty employees were regularly pasting client portfolio summaries into a consumer GenAI service to speed up quarterly review drafts. No one had acted maliciously. No one had read the terms of service closely either. The data left the perimeter, the provider's retention policy was unknown, and regulatory obligations around confidentiality had already been strained. The fix was not a ban; it was a sanctioned enterprise AI tier with logging, a clear acceptable-use policy, and a short training session built around the actual workflow people were trying to accelerate. Shadow AI is almost always a workflow problem wearing a compliance disguise.

The software supply chain has become an attack surface of its own. Modern development runs through agentic AI assistants—tools like Cursor, Claude Code, GitHub Copilot, and autonomous coding agents—which read from and write to repositories, call external APIs, and increasingly take multi-step actions on behalf of developers. That productivity unlock is real, and so is the new risk. Source code gets cloned into SaaS ecosystems for indexing, suggestion quality, or collaboration features. Credentials are hardcoded in a test branch surface inside a prompt. A compromised package or a poisoned model index can influence what the assistant suggests across hundreds of repositories. Supply-chain attacks in the last few years have shown how a single upstream compromise propagates to thousands of downstream consumers before detection is possible, and AI-driven development amplifies both the speed of propagation and the surface of exposure.

Workforce pressure is concentrated around skills, not seats. Cloud security, AI and ML security, identity engineering, and detection engineering remain the tightest specializations across most organizations. Teams can hold steady headcount and still struggle because only a small subset of people can investigate identity anomalies, validate cloud access patterns, or reason about a model's behavior under adversarial input. A skills gap also changes how programs succeed, because tools that require deep tuning and ongoing oversight need specialists who own outcomes rather than only operate dashboards. Many organizations now invest in training and internal enablement alongside technology, because operational speed depends on people who understand identity, cloud controls, incident response, and the specifics of AI behavior.

Governance moved from advisory to enforceable. The EU AI Act reached enforcement for prohibited practices and AI literacy in early 2025, with foundational governance provisions and general-purpose AI transparency obligations following later that year and high-risk system compliance phases extending into 2026. India's Digital Personal Data Protection Act is tightening obligations around consent, purpose limitation, and breach notification. The NIST AI Risk Management Framework, ISO/IEC 42001, sector rules under HIPAA, PCI DSS, DORA in the EU, and SEC cyber disclosure requirements in the US all now sit on the same calendar as delivery milestones. Documentation, oversight, and monitoring need to be planned early rather than added later under stress. Treating governance as product work, not paperwork, is what keeps a program defensible.

Key Data Points and Supporting Evidence

Five durable patterns anchor the conversation.

Threat pressure sits near a multi-year peak. Practitioners report a demanding environment driven heavily by social engineering, credential abuse, and cloud misconfiguration. Identity signals often appear across multiple systems, and attacker automation increases the odds that a weak signal becomes a major incident before manual analysis catches up.

Breach costs remain material even where they have plateaued. Global average breach cost hovers in the low-to-mid single-digit millions of dollars per incident. Recent reporting has connected lifecycle improvements to faster containment, with AI-assisted detection and response contributing to shorter lifecycles and lower losses.

AI adoption continues to outpace AI governance. Enterprise studies indicate that roughly four in five organizations run AI in production, while a far smaller portion treat AI as a governed asset with dedicated access controls, inventory, and oversight. The practical consequence is two parallel problems: sanctioned AI systems that need monitoring and evaluation, and unsanctioned AI usage that creates data exposure in places controls were never designed to cover.

Ransomware patterns shifted toward data theft. Enforcement disrupted several large brands, yet the ecosystem adapted through fragmentation and rebranding, and pressure moved toward exfiltration plus multi-layer extortion. Auxiliary tactics that increase urgency have expanded in parallel.

Regulatory momentum is now tied to deadlines globally. The EU AI Act, DPDPA in India, updated cyber disclosure rules in the US, and sectoral operational resilience rules in financial services together make governance a quarterly deliverable rather than an annual initiative.

Taking together, these data points describe a single operational view: threats scale, signals scatter, people and skills remain limited, and governance expectations tighten. AI becomes the capability that absorbs scale, and governance keeps that capability safe and auditable.

Insights and Practical Frameworks

The Expanded Threat Landscape: Different Surfaces, One Program

A useful shift for leaders is to stop thinking about cybersecurity as a list of tools and start thinking about it as a set of surfaces. It keeps reappearing in real incidents.

Code and application security is where most modern breaches now begin, whether through a vulnerable dependency, a mishandled secret, a broken authorization check, or logic that behaves safely in staging and unsafely in production. AI-assisted development accelerates shipping, which means defects—and defenders' response to them—compound faster.

Cloud security spans identity in the cloud, workload configuration, network posture, storage exposure, and the management plane. Misconfigurations still drive a meaningful share of breaches because change is constant and visibility is uneven.

Data security covers classification, access, retention, and movement. Shadow AI has made this surface both larger and less observable, because prompts and model outputs create new data flows that traditional DLP was not designed to see.

Identity security sits at the center of almost every serious incident. Credentials, tokens, session handling, privilege sprawl, and non-human identities such as service accounts and AI agents all belong here.

Endpoint, edge, and operational technology continue to matter. Endpoints remain the foothold; edge devices and OT systems extend the blast radius into the physical world, where compromise can create safety consequences that no pure IT incident produces.

AI itself is now a security surface. Prompt injections, indirect prompt injection via ingested content, model theft, training data poisoning, and agent privilege misuse are real categories with real tooling emerging around them. Programs that treat AI only as a defender miss half the picture.

The SOC sits at the center of this map. Its job is to correlate signals across all six surfaces, respond where needed, and escalate what carries a significant business impact. Early in the book, this broader view matters because later chapters go deep into individual surfaces, and the value becomes clearer when the relationships are already in mind.

AI as a Force Multiplier Across the Security Stack

AI's best work in security looks less like replacement and more like compression—of time, of context, and of the effort needed to see a story. It shows up differently in each surface.

Code security. AI assists with static and dynamic analysis, triaging vulnerability alerts by exploitability, summarizing diffs for security review, and flagging risky patterns such as hardcoded secrets, missing authorization checks, or unsafe deserialization. The same capability helps prioritize which of a thousand dependency alerts affect a reachable code path.

SOC operations. Event deduplication, enrichment with asset and identity context, correlation across email, endpoint, identity, and cloud, and readable case narratives turn a flood of alerts into a ranked queue of real cases. Generative summaries let an analyst open a case and see, in a paragraph, what happened, where, to whom, and why it is worth attention.

Cloud security. Posture tools with AI-driven prioritization highlight the misconfiguration that matters most, not just the longest list. Anomaly detection on cloud control-plane activity catches privilege escalations and unusual API patterns that signature rules miss.

Data security. Classification models identify sensitive content across unstructured stores. Behavior models flag unusual access to regulated data. Lineage tracking, increasingly AI-assisted, helps teams see where data ends up after it leaves its system of record—including when it leaves through a prompt.

Identity security. Risk-scored authentication, session anomaly detection, and privilege analytics turn a previously static surface into an adaptive one. Non-human identities—service accounts, CI/CD tokens, AI agent credentials—get treated with the scrutiny they have always deserved but rarely received.

AI security itself. Prompt inspection, output filtering, input and output classifiers, red-team harnesses, and runtime policies for autonomous agents apply security to the AI stack. This is the surface most programs are building from zero, and starting with inventory and access controls tends to pay back fastest.

The common thread is that AI helps people do what they already do, at a pace closer to the speed at which the attack is unfolding. Humans retain ownership of consequential decisions. Machines handle the volume, the context assembly, and the repeatable response steps.

The Secure SDLC, End to End: Build, Deploy, Run, Observe

Most programs still talk about "shifting left." The harder, more honest conversation is that security must hold across the whole lifecycle, because attackers do not care where left ends and right begins. A useful mental model is a loop: Plan, Build, Test, Deploy, Run, observe—with security and AI present at every stage, and runtime treated as first-class, not an afterthought.

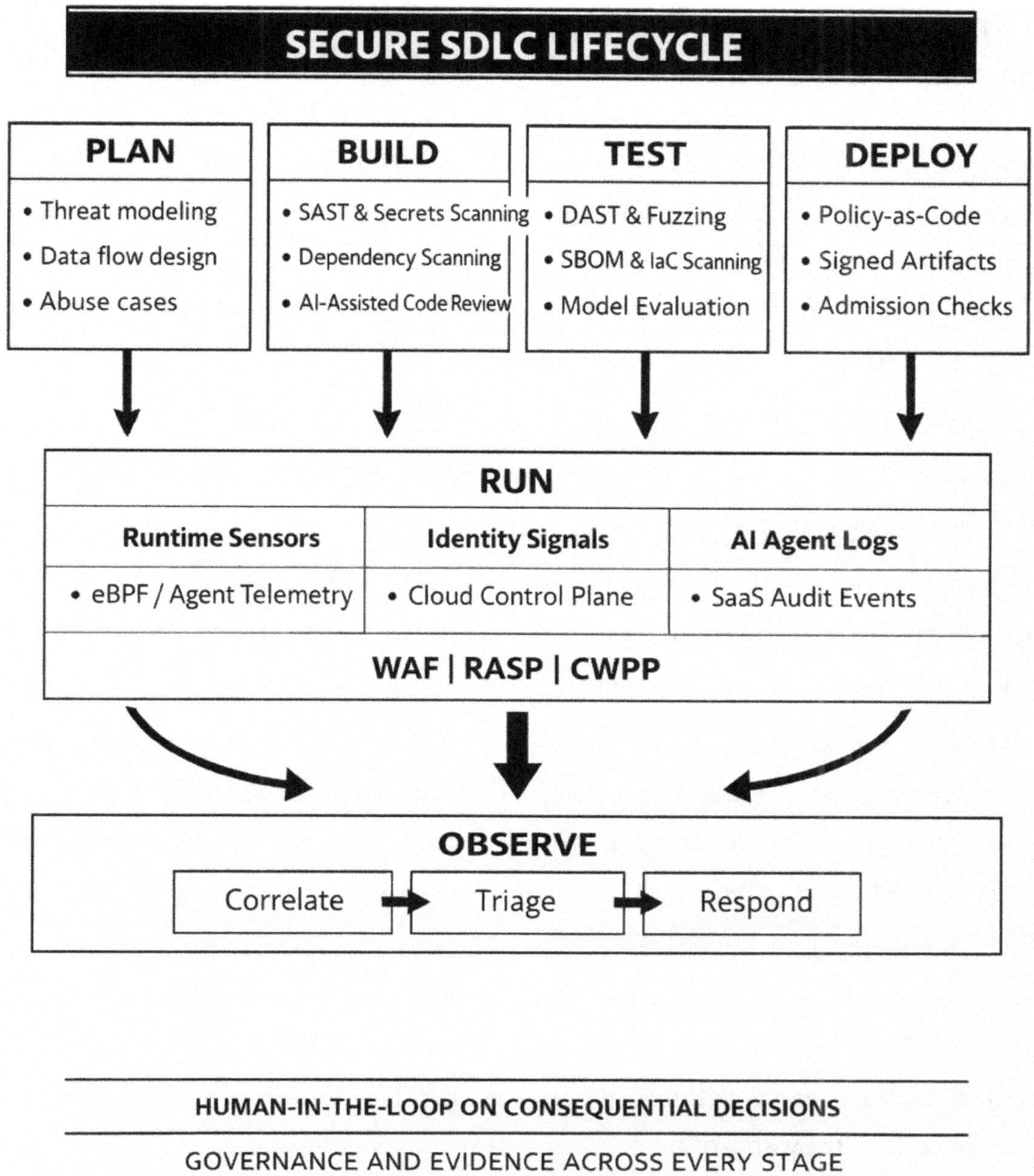

Figure 1.1: The Secure SDLC as a closed loop, with runtime sensors and observation feeding back into planning and build.

Plan is where threat models, data flow diagrams, and abuse-case thinking live. Skipping this stage is how organizations end up with a beautifully instrumented pipeline protecting the wrong asset.

Build is where AI-assisted development tools now sit permanently. Cursor, Claude Code, Copilot, and autonomous agents such as Devin-style systems accelerate coding and can, if governed, also raise code security posture by surfacing vulnerable patterns, missing input validation, and weak crypto. The risks—secrets leaked into prompts, intellectual property cloned into third-party indices, prompt injection through untrusted source material, and introduction of subtly vulnerable code patterns at scale—need explicit guardrails: sanctioned tools, enterprise tiers with data controls, repository allow-lists, code review that still happens, and model-generated code treated like any other untrusted input.

Test covers SAST, DAST, fuzzing, dependency scanning, SBOM generation, IaC policy checks, container and image scanning, and—for AI features—model evaluation harnesses that cover safety, robustness, and drift.

Deploy enforces policy-as-code at the admission boundary. Signed artifacts, signed SBOMs, and controlled deployment pipelines prevent a compromised build from becoming a compromised production system.

Run is where most of the action happens, and the most under-invested part of many programs. Runtime sensors—endpoint agents, eBPF-based probes, cloud workload protection, runtime application self-protection, identity telemetry, and SaaS audit events—give security teams the only honest view of what an application is doing in production. AI correlates these signals into coherent incident narratives.

Observe closes the loop. Findings from production feed back into planning and building. A vulnerability exploited in runtime becomes a pattern for SAST to catch earlier. An unusual SaaS API sequence becomes a policy rule. This feedback is where programs compound—or, if they are missing, where they stagnate.

Governance sits over the whole lifecycle. Who approved the deployment? Which model version is running? What data did it access? Those questions get answered by evidence collected automatically as part of the pipeline, not assembled by hand under audit pressure.

Runtime Sensors and Why Context Wins

Pre-production security finds patterns in code. Runtime security finds intent in behavior. The two are complementary, and the gap between them is where most serious incidents now live.

A vulnerability that is reachable in theory may be blocked by a configuration in production. A dependency that looked safe in testing may be invoked with adversarial input in the real world. A permission that looked fine in staging may, combined with a sibling permission granted six months later, allow a privilege escalation nobody modeled. Runtime sensors see these interactions because they observe the actual state, the actual identity using it, and the actual data flowing through it.

AI adds context to that telemetry in three practical ways. First, it groups related events into cases that tell a story rather than a stream. Second, it enriches events with information humans would otherwise fetch manually—asset criticality, identity privilege, recent configuration changes, and related vulnerabilities. Third, it learns what "normal" looks like for a workload, a user, or a service account, so deviations surface early. The combination is what lets a small team watch a large estate without drowning.

Human-in-the-Loop, Human-on-the-Loop, Human-out

Not every decision needs a human, and not every decision should be automated. A useful three-tier model keeps teams honest.

Human-in-the-loop means the AI recommends, and a human approves before action. This belongs to destructive or irreversible steps: isolating a production domain controller, revoking privileged access at scale, freezing customer accounts, blocking executive mailboxes, and locking build pipelines.

Human-on-the-loop means the AI acts and a human supervises, with the ability to intervene. This fits reversible or narrow actions where speed matters: auto-quarantining a single suspect endpoint, requiring step-up authentication on an anomalous login, suspending a suspicious session, and enriching a ticket with context.

Human-out-of-the-loop means fully automated action inside a tightly bounded scope, with observability and a kill switch. This fits high-confidence, low-blast-radius steps: blocking a known-malicious indicator, killing a clearly malicious process on a contained endpoint, and auto-expiring a token flagged as leaked.

The model matters because the wrong placement creates real harm. Full automation on a high-impact action creates outages. Human-in-the-loop on every action creates bottlenecks that the attacker exploits. Mature programs publish where each tool sits on this spectrum and review those placements as trust and evidence accumulate.

Business Impact and ROI: Metrics Leaders Can Defend

Speed converts into business value because faster detection and response reduce downtime, customer impact, regulatory exposure, and recovery cost. Leaders hold that conversation is better when the numbers are concrete. The table below shows indicative improvements we have seen in programs that combined AI-assisted detection and response with disciplined fundamentals. The specific numbers will vary; the shape is recognizable.

Metric	Baseline (pre-AI)	After 12 months	Business impact
Mean time to detect (MTTD)	8 – 24 hours	15 – 60 minutes	Earlier containment, smaller blast radius
Mean time to respond (MTTR)	24 – 72 hours	2 – 6 hours	Less downtime, lower recovery cost
Alerts per analyst per day	150 – 200	40 – 70	Lower fatigue, higher investigation quality
False positive rate	55 – 70%	15 – 25%	More trust in automation, faster triage
Phishing click-through (simulated)	18 – 22%	3 – 6%	Fewer credential-theft incidents
Critical vuln remediation SLA	30 – 45 days	7 – 14 days	Narrower exploit windows
Privileged session anomalies contained	Unmeasured	85 – 95% within 1 hr.	Harder lateral movement

Lifecycle metrics are the first lens. Avoided breach cost is the second—benchmarking against current global averages and internal incident frequency, with conservative assumptions documented openly, giving leaders a defensible ROI story. Analyst productivity, identity risk reduction, and coverage of crown-jewel assets round out the picture.

Inevitable Adoption, and Why Discipline Is the Differentiator

Attacker innovation continues at pace, and defender adoption is no longer optional. The edge does not come from having AI. It comes from the discipline around it—goal-anchored pilots tied to specific targets such as a fifty-percent MTTR reduction in a named domain, transparent governance aligned to applicable regulatory frameworks, documented human-oversight boundaries, and continuous evaluation against drift and evasion. Programs that treat AI as infrastructure—inventoried, monitored, governed, retired when it stops earning its place—outperform programs that treat it as a set of features.

Case Studies

Case Study 1: GenAI Phishing and Deepfake Surge

A multinational organization sees daily phishing volume climb from dozens to hundreds of messages. Attempts impersonating senior executives arrive with native tone and clean language, and some are reinforced by convincing deepfake voice calls authorizing urgent wire transfers. Targeting concentrates on finance and vendor operations, functions that handle high transaction volumes and face pressure to act quickly.

The SOC deploys AI-driven email defenses that combine linguistic modeling with sender behavior analysis and identity signal correlation, including mailbox rule changes and atypical login geographies. High-risk messages enter quarantine with analyst review lanes for sensitive mailboxes. Authentication is strengthened in high-risk workflows, vendor bank change controls are tightened, and user simulations are aligned with real executive and finance patterns.

After tuning, the organization filters roughly ninety-five percent of malicious email before inbox delivery. Simulated click-through rates fall from about twenty percent to below five percent across two quarters. Multiple near-miss business email compromise attempts are stopped before payment, and the highest-risk event—a CFO deepfake paired with a forged vendor domain and a realistic invoice trail—is intercepted before funds move, averting a six-figure loss.

The lesson is practical: attacker automation increases both scale and credibility, and defenders need machine-speed defenses that correlate signals across systems while preserving oversight for decisions with significant business impact.

Case Study 2: Shadow AI and the Source Code That Went Public

A mid-sized software company notices that a competitor's recent product release looks strikingly similar to an internal project still months from launch. An investigation begins, and the trail leads back to a team of developers who had been using a browser-based AI coding assistant without enterprise controls. The assistant indexed repository snippets to improve suggestion quality. Parts of proprietary modules were visible, through that index, to users outside the organization.

There was no malicious insider. There was no dramatic breach. There was a SaaS ecosystem that cloned code into places the security team did not have visibility into, an acceptable-use policy that had not been updated for AI-assisted development, and a productivity pressure that made the workflow attractive enough that developers did not ask.

The remediation combined three workstreams. The security team deployed an enterprise-tier AI coding assistant with contractual data protections, logging, and repository allow-lists. Legal added AI-specific language to contractor and employee agreements, aligned with evolving expectations under frameworks such as the EU AI Act and DPDPA. The engineering leadership ran a short enablement program showing developers how to use the sanctioned tool for exactly the tasks they had been doing in the shadow tool. Shadow AI usage measured at the proxy dropped by roughly ninety percent within a quarter.

The lesson is that intellectual property protection, in an era of agentic AI development, is a governance and tooling question more than a firewall question. The controls that matter are inventory, sanctioned alternatives, contractual terms, and developer enablement—applied before the next release cycle, not after.

Case Study 3: Cross-Surface Correlation Catches a Quiet Intrusion

A retail company with a large cloud footprint and a global workforce experience what could easily have become a major breach. The opening move is subtle: a finance analyst's session token is stolen through a malicious browser extension installed from a legitimate-looking productivity site. Traditional email filters never see the attack because nothing malicious arrives by email.

What the SOC sees is a collection of weak signals spread across surfaces. A login from an unusual ASN on the corporate identity provider. A small privilege assignment inside a cloud account. An API call pattern against an object storage bucket that contains customer export files. A single, low-volume egress flow to a domain registered two weeks earlier.

Each signal in isolation is noise. Correlated, they tell a coherent story: identity compromise, cloud privilege abuse, and early-stage data staging. The AI-driven detection platform groups the events into a single case, annotates the analyst view with identity privilege, asset criticality, and timeline, and recommends session revocation plus temporary privilege removal. The human-in-the-loop analyst approves both actions within minutes. The containment holds, the bucket is never exfiltrated, and the root-cause investigation identifies two other analysts with the same extension installed before any further damage occurs.

The lesson is that modern defense rarely comes from a single tool catching a single signal. It comes from correlation across surfaces, prioritization against business context, and fast but accountable human action.

Regulations and Standards: A Global View

Governance is now a design constraint, not an afterthought. The most material frameworks shaping AI-in-security programs worldwide include the following.

The EU AI Act introduces risk-tiered obligations across prohibited practices, high-risk systems, general-purpose AI transparency, and post-deployment monitoring, with phased enforcement through 2026. Even organizations outside the EU are affected when they serve EU residents or supply systems into EU markets.

India's Digital Personal Data Protection Act (DPDPA) establishes a consent-based framework for processing personal data, with explicit duties around purpose limitation, retention minimization, breach notification, and the rights of data principals. Security AI systems that ingest logs tied to individuals, user behavior data, or customer communications sit squarely inside its scope. Practical obligations include documented lawful basis for processing, clear retention windows for security telemetry, and breach reporting timelines that require mature incident response capabilities to be in place before an incident, not after. Organizations operating across India and other jurisdictions increasingly align their internal controls to the strictest applicable standard to simplify operations.

The NIST AI Risk Management Framework in the US provides a voluntary but widely adopted structure for identifying, measuring, and managing AI risk. ISO/IEC 42001 gives organizations a certifiable management system for AI, sitting alongside ISO 27001 for information security.

Sector-specific regulations continue to shape security AI use. HIPAA constrains the processing of protected health information by AI systems in healthcare. PCI DSS applies when AI touches payment data. DORA in the EU sets operational resilience expectations for financial services, including third-party risk and incident reporting. SEC cyber disclosure rules in the US require timely reporting of material cyber incidents, which raises the stakes on detection and investigation speed. GDPR remains the reference point for data protection across the EU, influencing how security telemetry and user-monitoring features are designed. Similar frameworks exist across the UK, Canada, Australia, Singapore, and the Gulf, and convergence is broadly in the direction of stronger accountability.

The practical leadership response is to build a single control set that maps to the applicable frameworks, maintain evidence as a by-product of daily operations, and treat documentation as something that exists now because an auditor, a regulator, or a customer may ask tomorrow.

KPIs to Track

KPIs work best when they tie AI deployment to risk reduction and operational efficiency, are reviewed on a consistent cadence, and carry clear ownership. The set below combines speed, quality, and coverage, with worked examples.

MTTD and MTTR by incident category. Establish baselines in hours or days, segment by vector such as phishing, identity compromise, cloud misconfiguration exploitation, and insider misuse, and target thirty-to-fifty-percent reductions in pilot domains. For example, identity-driven incidents moving from an eighteen-hour MTTD to under one hour in a year is a strong signal.

Incident load per analyst. Track closed cases per week, minutes per case, and the share of time spent collecting evidence versus taking action. An analyst moving from one useful alert in ten to one useful alert in two indicates that triage quality has improved, not just volume.

False positive rate by source. Measure precision and recall for email, endpoint, identity, and cloud separately. Pair quantitative metrics with analyst feedback so the system learns where recommendations add value. A cloud posture tool moving from a fifty-percent false-positive rate to fifteen percent after tuning is a recognizable milestone.

Coverage of critical assets and identities. Map crown-jewel systems and tier-0 identities, including non-human ones such as service accounts and AI agent credentials, and expand AI-enhanced monitoring toward full coverage. Seventy percent of crown jewels under adaptive authentication is a genuine milestone; forty percent is a gap worth naming.

Shadow AI exposure. Track sanctioned AI usage, observed unsanctioned AI usage at the proxy, and data loss events tied to AI tools. A program moving from unknown to measurable shadow AI is a meaningful maturity step on its own.

Secure SDLC health. Track critical vulnerability remediation SLA, percentage of services with SBOMs in production, percentage of deployments passing policy-as-code checks, and the count of secrets detected in repositories per month. A move from three hundred secret detections per month to under fifty is a tangible posture improvement.

Governance and evidence readiness. Track the percentage of AI systems in the AI inventory, percentage with a documented owner, percentage with defined human-oversight boundaries, and percentage with post-deployment monitoring live. A program that can answer "which AI systems influence security decisions, and who owns each one?" in ten minutes is in a different class from one that needs a week.

Risks and Guardrails

AI introduces new failure modes alongside speed and scale, so guardrails protect reliability, compliance, and trust. The examples below make the risks concrete.

Over-reliance risk. An analyst accepts an AI recommendation to isolate a server during a suspected ransomware event, and the server turns out to be a critical production database with no active attack. The guardrail is human-in-the-loop on destructive actions, reliability earned first in lower-risk workflows, and expansion of automation scope in phases with drift monitoring.

Data privacy and compliance risk. A security analytics platform ingests full email bodies to improve phishing detection. The data scope exceeds what the privacy notice described, and a regulator asks why. The guardrail is a routine data protection impact assessment, minimization of sensitive data in training and prompts, clear retention and access rules, and preference for private or controlled deployments for sensitive workloads.

Model security risk. A support assistant that summarizes customer tickets begins producing replies that reveal internal system details, after an attacker embeds instructions inside a ticket body. The guardrail is isolation of model contexts, filtering of untrusted inputs, restriction of tool access for autonomous actions, and logging of prompts and outputs for audit.

Shadow AI risk. A product team builds a customer-facing feature on top of a public AI API without telling security or legal. Customer data flows to a third party with unknown retention, the feature becomes a compliance issue, and the feature cannot be switched off without breaking the product. The guardrail is an AI inventory, a sanctioned AI platform with strong defaults, an intake process that is faster than the shortcut, and proxy-level visibility into unsanctioned AI traffic.

IP and code leakage through agentic development. A developer pastes a proprietary algorithm into a consumer AI coding assistant to debug a subtle edge case. The snippet becomes part of an index, and a month later, a similar pattern appears in a public output. The guardrail is sanctioned enterprise tooling with contractual data protections, repository allow-lists, developer enablement on sanctioned workflows, and updated employment and contractor terms covering AI-assisted development.

Bias and transparency risk. An insider-risk model flags a disproportionate share of a particular team because the training data over-represented incidents from that team's prior structure. The guardrail is fairness testing across subgroups, explainability requirements, human review before adverse action, and audit artifacts from vendors and internal systems.

Integration and change management risk. A new detection platform runs in parallel with the old one for two weeks, finds twenty additional incidents, and then gets decommissioned because the SOC does not have the capacity to triage the uplift. The guardrail is phased pilots with observation before enforcement, updates to standard operating procedures, training on new workflows, and feedback loops that tune thresholds and evidence quality.

Cost and benefit risk. A GPU-heavy anomaly detection system exceeds its cloud budget by a factor of three in its first month because all telemetry is analyzed rather than only what matters. The guardrail defines pilot targets, quantifies avoided cost against breach benchmarks, and monitors data scope and runtime usage with sampling or rate limits where appropriate.

Ethical use risk. A productivity-monitoring capability gets repurposed as insider-risk detection without clear employee communication, triggering trust damage and regulatory attention. The guardrail is scoped use cases, clear communication, restricted repurpose without review, and alignment with corporate values and local norms.

Executive Takeaways

- **AI is no longer optional, and neither is discipline.** The edge comes from the fundamentals around AI—identity, telemetry, patching, inventory—more than from any single tool.
- **Think in surfaces, not tools.** Code, cloud, data, identity, endpoint, OT, and AI each need explicit attention. The SOC correlates with them.
- **Shadow AI is already inside the perimeter.** Treat it as a workflow and governance problem with sanctioned alternatives, inventory, and enablement.
- **Secure SDLC must cover runtime.** Build-time controls matter; runtime sensors and behavioral context are where real attacks are caught. Close the feedback loop back into design.
- **Be explicit about human-in-the-loop placement.** Destructive actions need approval. Reversible actions can run with supervision. High-confidence, low-blast-radius actions can be fully automated with a kill switch.
- **Governance is a product, not paperwork.** The EU AI Act, DPDPA, NIST AI RMF, ISO/IEC 42001, and sector rules together make evidence a daily deliverable. Build once to the strictest applicable standard.
- **Measure what matters and publish it.** MTTD, MTTR, false positive rate, crown-jewel coverage, shadow AI exposure, SSDLC health, and governance readiness—reviewed on a cadence—are the honest signals.
- **Treat AI as infrastructure.** Inventory it, monitor it, govern it, and retire it when it stops earning its place. A program that can answer "which AI systems influence security decisions, and who owns each one?" in ten minutes is a program built to hold.

End-of-Chapter Reflection Questions

- Can your organization list every AI system that influences a security decision, and name its owner, in under ten minutes?
- If you measured shadow AI traffic at the egress proxy today, what would you expect to find—and what would you do with that data in the first thirty days?
- Which of the six surfaces (code, cloud, data, identity, endpoint/OT, AI itself) is your weakest, and which is the best instrumented?
- Where exactly does human-in-the-loop end and human-on-the-loop begin in your current playbooks? Is that boundary documented, or implicit?
- Which agentic AI development tools are in use by your engineering teams, and what controls are in place to prevent source code and secrets from leaving the perimeter through them?
- How does your runtime telemetry feed back into design and build decisions—and what is the longest-running unaddressed feedback signal from production right now?
- If a regulator asked you today how an AI-driven security decision was made on a specific date for a specific individual, could you answer with evidence produced automatically, or would you assemble it by hand?
- Which three KPIs, if you started publishing them monthly to the executive team, would sharpen the program over the next year?

Chapter 2

ARTIFICIAL INTELLIGENCE BASICS FOR SECURITY PROFESSIONALS

The Day "AI" Stopped Being a Buzzword

A lot of leaders entered cybersecurity through policy, risk, audit, operations, or IT, and then found the word "AI" sitting in every vendor pitch, board deck, and incident review. That can feel awkward, because security already carries enough jargon, and nobody wants to approve a major investment while relying on half-understood definitions.

This chapter solves that problem in plain terms. It gives you a working understanding of the core ideas that appear across modern security AI tools, so you can evaluate them with confidence, ask sharper questions, and set realistic expectations for your team. The six surfaces from Chapter 1—code, cloud, data, identity, endpoint, and OT, and AI itself—all draw on the same underlying vocabulary, and getting that vocabulary right once saves repeated confusion later.

The key promise of AI in security is scale. Machines process telemetry volumes and pattern spaces that no human team can, and they connect clues across logs, email, endpoint activity, identity events, and cloud signals with speed that helps defenders move before attackers finish their sequence. The key limitation is equally simple: AI learns patterns from data, and those patterns mislead when data is biased, incomplete, or outdated—and when people treat a model output as a final verdict rather than a recommendation.

By the end of this chapter, terms like machine learning, deep learning, NLP, generative AI, foundation model, agent, agentic AI, MCP, and AI red-teaming should feel familiar. You should also understand why accuracy alone never tells the full story in security, and why deployment choices—public model versus private, model alone versus agent with tool access—change your risk profile as much as the model itself.

A Working Taxonomy: Where Each Term Fits

AI is not one thing. It is a family of techniques with overlapping boundaries. A compact taxonomy keeps the rest of the chapter navigable.

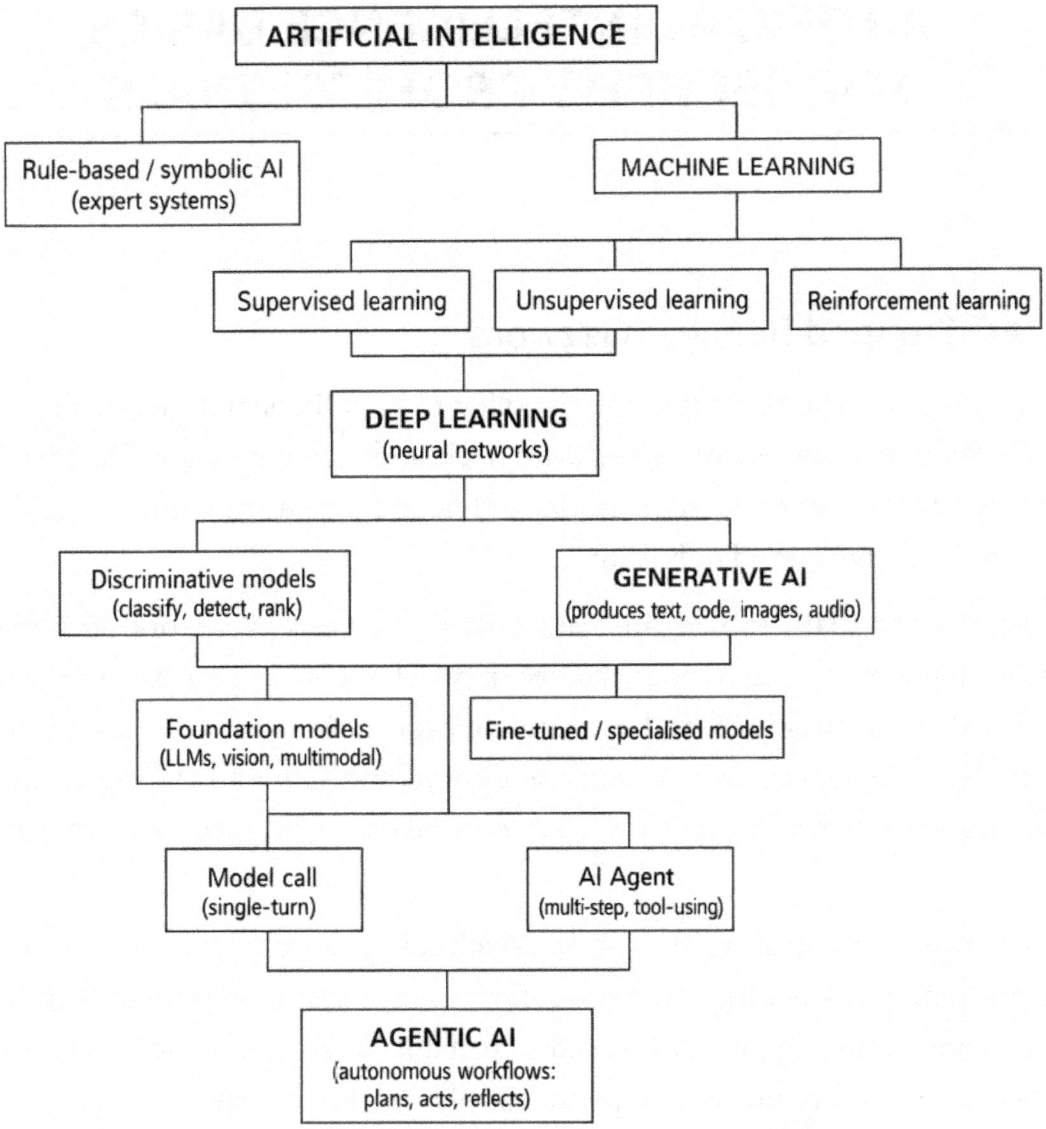

Figure 2.1: A working taxonomy for AI in security. Boundaries are fuzzy; the goal is orientation, not strict classification.

A few orientation notes. Rule-based systems are not usually called AI today, but much of security tooling still runs on rules, and that is fine—rules are deterministic, auditable, and fast. Machine learning earns its place when patterns are too numerous or too subtle for rules. Deep learning is a sub-family of machine learning that happens to dominate modern results on unstructured data. Generative AI is a use of deep learning where the output is new content rather than a class label. Agents and agentic AI add the dimension of action—the system not only answers, but it also decides and does.

Key Properties Leaders should Internalize

Five properties of AI systems matter more than any specific technique.

AI systems have error rates in both directions. False positives consume analyst time. False negatives create missed incidents. There is no configuration that eliminates both; the question is where the trade-off lives and whether it matches your risk tolerance.

Training data is destiny. Biased or outdated data produces blind spots. A phishing detector trained on last year's lures misses this year's style. A fraud model trained on a narrow demographic misses fraud that does not look like the training set.

Precision and recall matter more than accuracy. A model that says "all clear" on every input can hit 99 percent accuracy in a quiet environment and still miss every attack. Precision (how many alerts were real) and recall (how many real attacks were caught) tell an honest story.

Treat AI output like the recommendation of a fast, pattern-hungry junior analyst. Fast, tireless, good at noticing—still needs oversight and context. This framing keeps expectations grounded.

Deployment choices change the risk profile as much as the model. A locally hosted open model and a public frontier model solving the same problem produce different data flow, confidentiality, and regulatory consequences. The model matters; so does where it runs and who else can see what you send it.

Insights and Practical Frameworks

Machine Learning 101

Machine learning learns from historical data and predicts new inputs. A straightforward security example: a model classifying network connections as benign or malicious, trained on labeled examples of both. The model picks up patterns—unusual port combinations, payload sizes, timing—that are tedious to describe as rules.

The detail that matters for leaders sits in the training data. Representative data with recent attack patterns yields strong models. Biased or outdated data yields blind spots. Teams that collect incident outcomes, enrich logs, and maintain data governance have a durable advantage because their models keep learning from the environment they operate in, not from a frozen snapshot.

Supervised vs Unsupervised: Known Threats vs Unknown Threats

Supervised learning uses labeled outcomes—"legitimate" or "attack." It works well for threat types you already understand and can label reliably. A phishing classifier trained on millions of labeled emails is a supervised model.

Unsupervised learning finds structure without labels. It clusters user behavior, groups similar events, and flags outliers—which is how it surfaces compromised accounts or insider misuse even when you have no label for the exact scenario. Most modern SOC tools combine both: supervised for what the organization already understands, unsupervised for anomaly hunting, often packaged as UEBA.

Reinforcement learning, a third branch, shows up less often in security but is worth naming. It learns through trial and feedback and appears in adaptive defense systems that adjust policies based on outcomes.

Deep Learning: Power, Opacity, Trade-offs

Deep learning uses neural networks with many layers and performs well on unstructured data—text, images, audio, packet payloads, and long sequences of system calls. In security, it appears in malware classification from binary features, voice analysis for deepfake detection, and visual analysis for OCR on phishing images.

The trade-off is explainability. Deep models can reach high accuracy and can be difficult to explain. If a tool flags a senior executive's account as compromised or a critical production system as malicious, the organization will want understandable reasoning, not only a score. Many leaders treat explainability as a procurement requirement—particularly in regulated environments and high-impact use cases—either by choosing simpler models where they suffice or by requiring explainability tooling for the deep ones.

NLP and Language Models in Security

Natural Language Processing works with human language. In security, it contributes in three recurring ways. It turns threat intelligence reports into structured alerts by extracting entities and actions. It powers security assistants that let analysts ask questions of logs in plain language. And it drives content-based phishing detection that catches messages that keyword rules miss.

Modern NLP is increasingly built on large language models (LLMs). These models produce fluent, confident text, which is useful, and which also means confident errors slip through easily. Hallucination—the model producing plausible-sounding content that is not grounded in fact—is not a bug that gets patched away. It is an intrinsic property of the technique. Security teams treat LLM output as acceleration for investigation, documentation, and triage, with verification preserved for high-impact actions. Retrieval-augmented generation (RAG), where the model answers based on retrieved documents rather than its own parameters, reduces hallucination for factual queries and is the pattern behind most usable security assistants.

Generative AI and Foundation Models

Generative AI produces new content—text, code, images, audio, and structured data. A foundation model is a large model pretrained on broad data that can be adapted to many tasks. LLMs like GPT-4-class, Claude, Gemini, and open models like Llama are foundation models. Vision and multimodal foundation models do the same across images and audio.

For security, three patterns matter most. Generation—drafting incident summaries, writing detection rules, producing user-facing explanations. Extraction—pulling structured facts from messy inputs like threat reports, emails, or ticket threads. Reasoning over retrieved context—the RAG pattern, where the model reasons over logs, documentation, or tickets you hand it.

Two adaptation choices matter. Prompting (and its richer cousins like few-shot prompting and RAG) gets you results quickly without touching model weights. Fine-tuning trains the model on domain-specific data and changes its behavior more permanently. Most enterprise security deployments start with prompting and RAG; fine-tuning earns its place where the domain is specialized and the volume justifies the cost and governance overhead.

Public vs Private Models: Deployment Choices

This distinction matters for every security leader because it determines where data goes.

Public (hosted) models are accessed over the internet through a provider API or consumer interface. You send prompts, the provider processes them, and you get responses. The provider sees your input. Retention, logging, training-on-your-data, and jurisdiction depend on the contract—consumer tiers often retain and train on inputs by default, enterprise tiers usually do not, but the terms change and need to be read carefully.

Private (self-hosted or dedicated) models run inside your infrastructure—on-premises, in your virtual private cloud, or in a single-tenant managed environment. You control the data flow. You also control the cost, the scaling, the patching, and the governance overhead.

Hybrid patterns are common in practice. A frontier model accessed over a zero-retention enterprise API for general reasoning, a smaller private model for sensitive data extraction, and a policy layer that decides which route a given request takes based on data sensitivity.

The practical leadership decision: what data can never leave, what data can leave with controls, and what data is low risk. Map the use case to one of those three buckets, and the deployment choice usually follows. Shadow AI, from Chapter 1, is almost always a signal that this mapping has not been made visible to the teams who need it.

AI Agents and Agentic AI: What Changes When AI Acts

A model call is a single exchange: input in, output out, the world is unchanged. An AI agent is a system where the model can take actions—call a tool, query a database, send an email, modify a file, execute a command—and use the results to decide what to do next. Agentic AI is the broader pattern of agents that plan, act, reflect, and iterate toward a goal with minimal human intervention.

This sounds like a small step. It is not. The security consequences are material.

A model call leaks data into a prompt and a response. An agent does that, and can also execute code, make API calls with credentials, and modify systems. A malicious prompt that would be an annoyance against a model call can become a real-world action against an agent. Prompt injections covered later in this chapter and in depth in Chapter 7—becomes a remote-action vulnerability rather than a text-generation nuisance.

The practical implications shape how programs govern agents from day one. Blast radius matters: the scope of what an agent can touch defines the worst-case incident, and agents should receive the minimum tools, credentials, and data they need. Non-human identity applies agent credentials, which are identities, subject to rotation, scoping, and monitoring like any service account, and arguably more tightly. Observability matters: every tool call, input, and output should be logged with enough context to reconstruct what happened and why. Human-in-the-loop placement from Chapter 1 applies directly: destructive or irreversible agent actions belong behind human approval until reliability is proven for that specific action in that specific environment.

Examples from current practice include developer agents (Cursor, Claude Code, Devin-class systems) that read and write code; SOC investigation agents that pivot across logs; customer-support agents that access ticketing systems; and workflow agents that orchestrate across SaaS tools. Each adds value; each changes the threat model.

MCP: How Agents Connect to the Real World

The Model Context Protocol (MCP) is an open standard that emerged in late 2024 and has become the default way AI applications connect to tools, data sources, and other systems. Think of it as a common adapter: instead of every AI application building custom integrations for every tool, MCP servers expose capabilities in a standard way, and any MCP-compatible AI client can use them.

The security team's interest in MCP is simple: it sits between the AI agent and the rest of the estate, so it is squarely on the threat path.

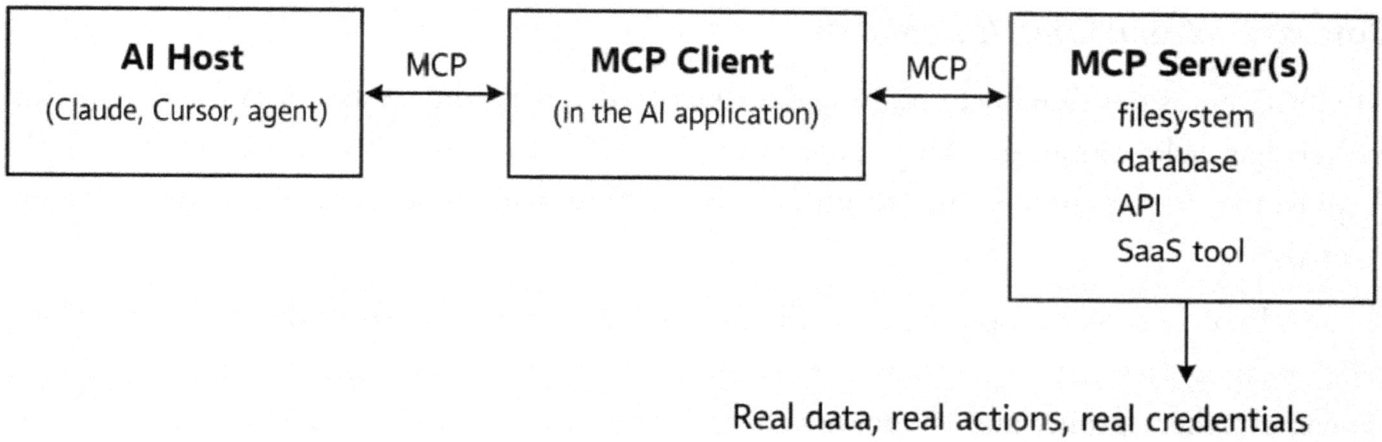

Figure 2.2: MCP connects AI hosts to tools and data. The MCP server is where credentials, data, and actions live.

Four security risks deserve explicit attention.

Untrusted tool connections. An MCP server from an unvetted source can do anything the protocol allows, which includes reading files, making API calls, and executing commands. Connecting an MCP server is closer to installing a browser extension with broad permissions than to adding a read-only data source.

Prompt injection via MCP resources. When an agent reads content through an MCP server—a document, a ticket, a webpage—instructions hidden in that content can hijack the agent's next action. This is the indirect prompt injection pattern applied to the MCP data path.

Credential exposure to agents. MCP servers often hold credentials for the systems they connect to. A compromised MCP server or an agent that leaks its context can expose those credentials to prompts, logs, or downstream systems.

Supply-chain risk in MCP servers. MCP servers themselves are software. They have dependencies, maintainers, and update mechanisms. A malicious or compromised MCP server is a supply-chain incident waiting to happen.

Defensive patterns follow these risks. Maintain an inventory of sanctioned MCP servers. Require signed, versioned releases and review updates before deployment. Scope credentials tightly—per-server, per-purpose, short-lived where possible. Apply input and output filtering on the MCP path to catch injected instructions and data exfiltration. Log all MCP calls as high-value security telemetry. Treat MCP servers as non-human identities with their own lifecycle. And when an MCP server sits between an agent and a sensitive system, place human-in-the-loop on the destructive actions.

Data as Fuel, and What It Demands

AI effectiveness ties directly to training data quality, diversity, and freshness. A fraud detection model that lacks mobile-banking fraud examples will miss mobile fraud disproportionately. A phishing model trained on English-only corpora will underperform on multilingual campaigns.

Two habits keep programs healthy. The first is access to high-quality, diverse data—across roles, geographies, and operational variation. The second is continuous learning: threats evolve, attackers probe, and models need updates with new data regularly. Many security AI products include continuous retraining or cloud threat feeds, and this only works when the organization side maintains data governance—collecting and labeling outcomes so the system improves.

When teams treat data as a first-class asset, AI systems improve month by month. When teams treat data as an afterthought, models drift away from reality. This is the single most reliable differentiator between programs that scale and programs that stall.

Limits and Misconceptions

AI finds patterns, and correlation misleads when context is missing. A developer doing something unusual but approved can look like an anomaly. A legitimate marketing campaign can look like a phishing pattern. Context—who the user is, what the project allows, what day it is—is what turns a pattern into a judgment.

Attackers also attempt to confuse AI directly, through adversarial examples, data poisoning, and prompt injections. These are covered in depth in Chapter 7.

At the leadership level, the habit that matters most is measuring error rates in your environment, not trusting a vendor lab number. A “95% accuracy” marketing claim rarely survives contact with production telemetry. Treat AI like a junior analyst who works at machine speed—tireless pattern detection and summarization, with oversight, training, and review that prevent preventable mistakes.

OWASP Top 10 for LLM Applications: Reference Card

The OWASP Top 10 for LLM Applications is the most widely used framework for LLM-specific risks. The table below is a quick reference; each item deserves deeper treatment in design reviews.

Table 2.1: OWASP Top 10 for LLM Applications, with one-line defenses. Treat this as a design-review checklist, not a completion target.

#	Risk	One-line defense
LLM01	Prompt Injection	Treat all inputs, including retrieved content, as untrusted; separate system and user context; filter known injection patterns.
LLM02	Sensitive Information Disclosure	Minimize sensitive data in prompts and training; apply output filtering; avoid returning raw data the user should not see.
LLM03	Supply Chain	Inventory models, adapters, datasets, and MCP servers; verify provenance and signatures; monitor for drift and tampering.
LLM04	Data and Model Poisoning	Validate training and fine-tuning data; sandbox untrusted contributions; test models against known poisoning signatures.
LLM05	Improper Output Handling	Treat model output as untrusted before passing it to code, shells, or downstream systems; sanitize, validate, parameterize.
LLM06	Excessive Agency	Grant agents the minimum tools, permissions, and credentials required; require human approval for destructive actions.
LLM07	System Prompt Leakage	Do not place secrets in system prompts; assume system prompts can be extracted; design controls that hold even if leaked.
LLM08	Vector and Embedding Weaknesses	Protect vector stores with access controls; watch for embedding-based data leakage; validate embeddings from untrusted sources.
LLM09	Misinformation	Ground outputs in retrieved, cited sources; label confidence; preserve human verification for consequential decisions.
LLM10	Unbounded Consumption	Apply rate limits, token budgets, timeout policies, and cost monitoring; protect against denial-of-wallet attacks.

AI Red-Teaming: Testing Before Attackers Do

Traditional security red teams test networks, applications, and people. AI red teams test models and AI systems. The mandate overlaps with classical red-teaming—find weaknesses, demonstrate impact, drive remediation—and the techniques are different.

An AI red team looks for failure modes that matter in production. Prompt injection through user input and through retrieved content. Jailbreaks that bypass safety training. Data extraction attacks that coax sensitive data from the model or its retrieval layer. Model inversion and membership inference attacks against sensitive training sets. Tool-use abuse, where an agent is manipulated into making harmful API calls. Supply-chain manipulation of models, datasets, and MCP servers. Denial-of-wallet attacks that drive up inference cost. Unsafe outputs in edge cases that surface rarely but predictably.

Roles and composition. Effective AI red teams combine three backgrounds: classical offensive security, machine-learning engineering, and domain experts from the application area (healthcare, finance, customer service, code). The combination matters because AI failures are often domain-specific. A jailbreak that is theoretical in a general context can be material when applied to a medical chatbot or a code-review agent.

Cadence. Pre-launch red-team review should be a gate for any consequential AI deployment, not an afterthought. Post-launch, red-teaming runs on a cadence—monthly for high-risk systems, quarterly for most others—with ad-hoc rounds triggered by model updates, new integrations, or newly published attack techniques.

What they test. The model itself, the surrounding application, the retrieval layer, the tool integrations, and the human workflow around it. Testing just the model in isolation misses the failure modes that matter most in production.

How findings flow back. Findings feed into three places: the model and prompt design (patch the specific vector), the surrounding controls (add input/output filters, tighten tool permissions, add human-in-the-loop on risky actions), and the detection stack (add telemetry so the pattern is visible if it happens in production). A red-team finding that produces only "we will train the model not to do that" is almost always insufficient—defense-in-depth around the model is what holds when the model fails.

Small organizations often cannot staff a dedicated AI red team. Two workable alternatives: partner with external AI red-teaming specialists on a scheduled cadence, and adopt open red-teaming tooling (Microsoft PyRIT, Meta Purple Llama, community jailbreak collections) to run structured probes against sanctioned AI systems. Either approach beats the common default of no structured adversarial testing at all.

Case Studies

Case Study 1: A Machine Learning Malware Classifier

A cybersecurity startup builds a machine learning malware detector to supplement traditional antivirus. They collect a dataset of one million files, split evenly between known malware and clean software, and train a supervised ensemble model. The model learns to differentiate malware through file structure, API call frequency, and embedded strings.

In testing, the model achieves 98% detection on known malware, comparable to signature-based antivirus. The more interesting result appears with variants: the system catches new malware strains an average of two days before antivirus signatures are available. In one case, a new ransomware family is flagged based on behavioral similarity to known ransomware, giving incident responders a meaningful head start.

The metrics are strong and realistic rather than perfect. Precision measures around 95%, keeping false positives manageable. Recall on genuinely novel malware is around 90%, meaning some new or well-camouflaged samples still slip through.

Guardrails are built into training. Benign files span a wide variety of common software, so the model avoids mislabeling them. The model retrains monthly with newly collected malware samples to stay current. For one deploying customer, an insurance firm, the malware incident rate drops by 30% in a year, and SOC analysts report the alerts are high-confidence—a signal that the system is filtering noise rather than producing it.

The executive lesson is straightforward: supervised ML generalizes from examples, catching variants of known threats, and that matters as attackers produce polymorphic malware at scale. The leadership follow-up question becomes what data feeds the model, how often it retrains, how it handles drift, and how the tool supports analyst verification when it flags an item.

Case Study 2: Unsupervised Login Anomaly Detection

A corporate network runs unsupervised clustering on user login events. The system has no label for "bad." It groups similar behavior—office staff logging in during business hours from corporate devices, IT administrators logging in at varied hours from VPN, and learning each pattern.

A login appears that fits none of the clusters: an accountant signs in at 3 AM from an unusual geography. The system flags it as an outlier. The security team treats it as a possible compromise, reviews context, and confirms credential theft through a session replay and a recent phishing click. Containment begins within the hour.

The insight is that unsupervised AI surfaces unknown unknowns—patterns no one labeled in advance. This complements supervised systems that focus on known bad, and it is why UEBA has become standard in modern SOC tooling.

There is an operational reality worth naming. A legitimate event can look like an anomaly: an employee traveling abroad, a developer working a late release window, a contractor onboarded yesterday. Human judgment and context (travel data, HR records, recent change tickets) refine the conclusion. This is why AI tools need workflow integration—somewhere to store context, a mechanism for analysts to label outcomes, and the ability to learn from those outcomes so noise decreases over time rather than staying flat.

KPIs to Track

AI programs are strengthened when teams measure performance in ways that link directly to security outcomes.

Model precision and recall. Track the percentage of AI alerts that were real issues and the percentage of real incidents AI caught. Targets like precision above 90% and recall above 85% on critical detection, with drift monitoring that signals aging models.

False positive reduction. Compare alert volumes before and after introducing AI in a workflow. A reduction from 100 alerts per day to 40 per day with equal or improved coverage is a measurable success and a trust signal.

Threat coverage. Map the categories the AI is responsible for detecting, then track whether incidents continue in those categories. Gaps become priorities.

Time saved in analysis. Ticket timing, workflow analytics, and periodic analyst surveys make productivity gains visible beyond detection metrics.

Training and evaluation freshness. Track how recently models retrained and when they were last evaluated against new test sets. Set a policy: no ML model stays in production beyond an agreed window without evaluation.

Agent-specific KPIs. For systems using agents, track tool-call volume by tool, successful versus blocked destructive actions, prompt-injection detection rate at input and output filters, and percentage of agent actions covered by human approval where required.

Risks and Guardrails

AI produces strong outcomes alongside predictable risks. Guardrails keep risks manageable and trust high.

Bias in models. Biased training data produces biased outputs. An insider-threat model trained mostly in cases from one demographic or department can produce unfair scrutiny patterns. The guardrail is bias testing across subgroups, diverse training data, and deliberate exclusion of sensitive attributes unless justified.

Overfitting and confidence inflation. A model that performs beautifully on historical data can struggle with new patterns. Train-test splits, cross-validation, and ongoing performance monitoring catch this; precision and recall drop trigger retraining.

Interpretability vs accuracy. Deep models can act like black boxes, creating risk for trust and compliance. The guardrail is simpler models where they suffice, explainability tooling where they do not, and documented reasoning for high-impact decisions.

Adversarial manipulation. Attackers craft inputs to evade detection or poison training data. Guardrails include input validation, layered detection so rules and behavior analytics catch what models miss, and the red-teaming cadence described earlier.

Resource and cost management. Training and inference consume computing and cloud spend, and costs can surprise without controls. Budget monitoring, sampling where appropriate, and rate limits prevent GPU-heavy workloads from becoming budget incidents.

Human expertise erosion. When teams rely too heavily on AI, analysts lose the habit of building intuition and validating evidence. Regular manual exercises, AI-off drills, and investigations performed without assistance keep the skill base alive.

These guardrails point to one operating principle: AI improves security when it sits inside disciplined workflows with evidence, measurement, and oversight.

Executive Takeaways

- **Vocabulary unlocks clarity.** ML for classification and prediction, deep learning for complex and unstructured data, NLP and LLMs for language, generative AI for content production, agents and agentic AI when the system takes action in the real world.
- **Deployment choices shape risk as much as the model.** Public, private, and hybrid patterns each have a place; the decision follows from data sensitivity and use case.

- **Agents are a qualitatively different risk profile.** Actions, not just text. Apply least-privilege tool access, non-human identity hygiene, observability, and human-in-the-loop on destructive steps.
- **MCP is how agents reach the real world.** Inventory MCP servers, vet sources, scope credentials, filter inputs and outputs, and logging everything.
- **OWASP Top 10 for LLM is a design-review anchor.** Use it as a checklist during system design, not a post-incident lookup table.
- **AI red-teaming earns its seat at the table.** Pre-launch gate for consequential systems, cadence post-launch, findings flow to model, controls, and detection—not just the model.
- **Data quality and freshness decide long-run performance.** Treat data as a first-class asset; treat outcome labeling as security work, not an optional activity.
- **Evaluate with the right metrics.** Precision, recall, false-positive reduction, agent-specific KPIs, and evaluation freshness tell the honest story. Accuracy alone does not.

End-of-Chapter Reflection Questions

- If a vendor pitches an "AI-powered" security product tomorrow, which three questions from this chapter will you ask first?
- For the AI systems currently influencing security decisions in your organization, which are public-hosted, which are private, and is that mapping documented?
- Which of your AI systems are agents—that is, they take actions—and do they have the least-privilege tool access and observability to match?
- If an attacker hid instructions in a document that one of your agents reads through MCP, what would happen next? Where would the defense activate?
- Has a structured AI red-team exercise ever been run against your sanctioned AI systems? If not, which system would you start with and why?
- Map each item in the OWASP Top 10 for LLM to a control you already have, a control you are missing, or a control that is partial. Which gap is most urgent?
- For every deployed model, can you state when it was last evaluated, what data it was trained on, and who owns its lifecycle? Where are the blanks?
- Which "AI-off drill" would most sharpen your SOC—and when was the last time one ran?

Chapter 3

CYBERSECURITY FUNDAMENTALS–THREATS, RISKS, AND THE CIA TRIAD

You Can't "AI" Your Way Around Fundamentals

AI has transformed modern security operations through faster detection, better correlation, and more efficient response workflows, and many teams now handle incident volumes that would have overwhelmed them a few years ago. Even with that progress, foundational cybersecurity hygiene still decides whether an organization resists common threats or becomes easy to breach. Incidents still begin with delayed patching, uneven MFA coverage, weak identity governance, porous segmentation, misconfigured cloud resources, and backups that look complete in dashboards and fail during an urgent restore.

This chapter sets the expectation for the rest of the book: AI strengthens security when it sits on a stable baseline. It brings speed, pattern recognition, and better signal connection across email, identity, endpoints, and cloud systems. It also depends on disciplined operations, because anomaly detection needs a reliable "normal," correlation needs consistent telemetry, and automation needs response actions that teams have rehearsed. When fundamentals vary widely, AI outputs become noisy, analyst trust drops, and leadership receives confusing signals even when the underlying product works well. Teams then spend energy debating whether the system is wrong instead of using it to move faster, and that debate can slow response during the moments when minutes matter most.

The goal here stays practical. Strengthen the foundation first, then apply AI to improve visibility and speed, so the organization gains measurable protection rather than louder alerts. When leaders treat fundamentals as non-negotiable work, AI becomes a force multiplier for teams already doing the basics well, and it also becomes a coach that highlights where the basics need tightening—patch gaps, privileged access sprawl, shadow AI tooling, misconfigured storage, systems that generate poor telemetry.

Fundamentals First: A Shared Language

Before moving deeper into AI-specific security capabilities, leaders benefit from a shared view of common threats and a shared language for what security protects. This chapter focuses on three anchors that scale well across teams and roles: a comprehensive list of attack vectors that spans the modern security landscape, the CIA triad extended with the pillars that the original formulation predates, and a small set of supporting models—AAA, zero trust, defense in depth, and practical risk framing—that practitioners reach for daily.

Confidentiality means preventing unauthorized access to information—customer data, financial records, product plans, employee details, credentials, training datasets, model weights. Integrity means ensuring data, systems, and model outputs remain accurate and unaltered, so operations rely on trustworthy records, configurations, and decisions. Availability means ensuring systems and services remain operational when employees, customers, and partners need them.

Two pillars that the original CIA triad predates now belong alongside it in practice. Privacy is the right of individuals to have control over how their personal data is collected, used, retained, and disclosed. It overlaps with confidentiality but is not identical—a system can be fully confidential from outsiders and still violate privacy through inappropriate internal use. Authenticity is the property that information and identities are genuine and verifiable—that a message really came from the claimed sender, that a model output really came from the authorized model, that a signed artifact really came from the claimed build pipeline. Non-repudiation, which ensures actions cannot be credibly denied after the fact, is closely related and sits at the intersection of integrity and authenticity.

These pillars together give leaders the vocabulary to connect technical events to business consequences. A breached CRM is a confidentiality incident. A tampered transaction log is an integrity incident. A ransomware outage is an availability incident. A model that quietly learned to return embedded training data is a privacy incident. A deepfake authorizing a transfer is an authenticity incident. Each category points to different controls and different response actions.

Key Data Points and Supporting Evidence

Four durable patterns explain why fundamentals deserve priority before organizations scale security AI broadly.

Phishing and social engineering remain the most common starting points for breaches. Reporting across major industry studies consistently places phishing in the majority of initial-access incidents, and the proportion has only grown as generative AI raises the quality of lures.

The strategic insight stays stable: email and identity remain high-value entry points, and controls that reduce successful phishing reduce downstream incident volume across every surface.

Unpatched vulnerabilities continue to drive a meaningful share of breaches. Recent reporting attributes roughly a third of breaches to exploitation of known, unpatched weaknesses. Patch discipline and asset management decide whether adversaries find easy footholds—and AI-driven prioritization matters most when a team has too many vulnerabilities to patch at once, which is nearly every team.

Cloud misconfiguration is now on equal footing with classical attack vectors. Patterns in major incident reports consistently point to public storage, overprivileged identities, unscoped API keys, and overly permissive security groups as root causes. The shift to multi-cloud and hybrid environments has widened the surface without widening most teams' visibility.

Identity-driven attacks have overtaken malware as the dominant mode of intrusion. Credential theft, session hijacking, token abuse, and privilege escalation now feature in most significant breaches—often without any traditional malware at all. This matches what Chapter 1 introduced: the old center of gravity has shifted from email-plus-endpoint to the full surface, with identity as the connective tissue.

These patterns guide where AI investment pays off early. If phishing and credential theft lead to many incidents, AI-assisted email filtering and identity analytics deserve focus. If unpatched vulnerabilities drive exploitation, AI-based prioritization and exploit-behavior detection deserve priority. If cloud misconfiguration is repeated, posture management with AI-driven ranking and runtime correlation becomes a natural investment. A practical program begins where attacks start, then extends into detection and response improvements that shrink containment time.

Insights and Practical Frameworks

The CIA Triad, Extended

The CIA triad becomes useful when it guides day-to-day decisions. AI contributes to each pillar in distinct ways, and those contributions strengthen when baselines stay consistent.

Confidentiality improves when AI models detect unusual access behavior and flag potential exfiltration patterns—unexpected queries against sensitive datasets, access from rare locations, unusual sequences of reads and exports. A concrete example: an AI model flags an HR database being queried late at night by an account outside HR, prompting session interruption and review before a mass export completes.

Integrity improves when AI monitors logs, file changes, and configuration updates to identify rare sequences that suggest tampering. Integrity failures often start with subtle edits—privileged policy changes, small modifications to files that support core operations, model weights replaced with a near-identical poisoned version. An AI anomaly detector can flag unusual event sequences even when the specific malware or attack signature is unfamiliar.

Availability improves when AI identifies early warning signs of service disruption. For ransomware, unusual file I/O patterns can signal encryption activity before spreading. For DDoS, ML-driven traffic classification can detect precursor patterns before a full flood, giving teams a window to mitigate before services degrade.

Privacy improves when AI is trained to recognize regulated data classes across unstructured stores and to flag access patterns that suggest misuse of legitimate permissions. In the Shadow AI pattern from Chapter 1, this is often where the first signal of data leaving the perimeter appears—not from a system compromise, but from legitimate users sending regulated data to an unsanctioned service.

Authenticity improves when AI supports deepfake detection in voice and video workflows, validates content provenance through analysis of metadata and signature trails, and strengthens verification in high-impact workflows such as vendor payment changes and executive approvals. Authenticity failures are often quiet—the recipient believes the message is genuine until a loss is discovered later.

These gains become meaningful only when identity controls, patch cycles, segmentation, and telemetry quality stay consistent. A team with a clean asset inventory, consistent logging, and clear ownership acts on AI findings immediately. A team with unknown assets and unclear owners loses time figuring out what the alert refers to.

Beyond CIA: AAA, Zero Trust, Defense in Depth

Three further models show up so often in mature programs that leaders benefit from knowing them by name.

AAA—Authentication, Authorization, Accounting. Authentication proves who someone (or what service) is. Authorization decides what they are allowed to do. Accounting records of what they did. Weaknesses in any of the three create security incidents. Weak authentication is credential theft. Weak authorization is privilege escalation and sprawl. Weak accounting is the inability to investigate, prove compliance, or learn from an incident. Modern IAM systems, which Chapter 6 covers in depth, strengthen all three.

Zero trust is the operating principle that no user, device, or service should be implicitly trusted because of network location or prior access. Every request is authenticated, authorized against the current context, and logged. This shifts security away from perimeter-based thinking toward continuous verification—and it is the only operating model that scales across cloud, SaaS, remote work, and non-human identities (including AI agents) at once.

Defense in depth is the layered approach that assumes any single control will occasionally fail. Multiple overlapping controls—preventive, detective, corrective—mean failure of one does not become compromised of the whole. The classic example: even with strong email filtering, MFA protects against credentials that slip through; even with MFA, endpoint detection catches malware delivered through another path; even with endpoint detection, segmentation and least privilege limit blast radius if something executes; even after execution, backups and recovery procedures determine how quickly operations resume. AI strengthens layered security by correlating signals across the layers—a capability humans cannot match at scale.

An example makes this concrete. An AI correlation engine links a minor firewall alert, a slight increase in database read loads on a sensitive system, a suspicious email received by an administrator, and an unusual login location for the same administrator a few hours later. Each signal alone is low risk. Together, they describe a coordinated intrusion spanning initial access, identity targeting, and data staging. This kind of multi-layer correlation is where AI earns its place—and it only works when the underlying layered controls are in place and feeding consistent data.

The Expanded Attack Vector Landscape

Attack vectors keep reappearing across industries, even as tooling and tactics evolve. The table below extends the traditional short list to cover the full modern landscape—across the six surfaces introduced in Chapter 1.

Table 3.1: Attack vectors across the six surfaces from Chapter 1, mapped to primary CIA impact. Categories overlap in practice; most real incidents span multiple vectors.

Attack Vector	Primary Surface	Primary CIA Impact	What Happens
Phishing and BEC	Endpoint / Identity	Confidentiality	Credential theft or malicious action via social engineering, often reinforced by deepfakes.
Credential Abuse and Session Hijack	Identity	Confidentiality, Integrity	Stolen credentials, tokens, or cookies grant direct access without malware.
Unpatched Vulnerability Exploitation	Code / Endpoint	Confidentiality, Integrity	Known weaknesses exploited before patch deployment enables footholds and privilege escalation.
Zero-Day Exploits	Code / Endpoint	Confidentiality, Integrity	Unknown vulnerabilities used before patches exist, often in high-value targets.
Cloud Misconfiguration	Cloud	Confidentiality, Availability	Public storage, over-privileged roles, open security groups, or management-plane weaknesses expose data and services.
API Abuse	Code / Cloud	Confidentiality, Integrity	Business logic flaws, broken authorization, excessive data exposure, or credential reuse against exposed APIs.
Ransomware and Destructive Malware	Endpoint / Cloud	Availability, Integrity	Encryption, wiping, or manipulation of systems paired with extortion over exfiltrated data.
Data Exposure and Privacy Breach	Data	Confidentiality, Privacy	Exposed datastores, over-shared SaaS files, unsanctioned AI tool usage (Shadow AI), or inappropriate internal access.
Insider Threats	Identity / Data	Confidentiality, Integrity	Misuse of legitimate access for exfiltration, sabotage, or policy violation, intentional or negligent.
Supply Chain Compromise	Code / Cloud / AI	Integrity, Confidentiality	Malicious updates, compromised packages, poisoned models or datasets, or trusted-vendor breaches.

Attack Vector	Primary Surface	Primary CIA Impact	What Happens
DDoS	Cloud / Endpoint	Availability	Traffic floods overwhelm services, sometimes serving as cover for concurrent intrusion activity.
AI-Specific Attacks	AI	Integrity, Confidentiality, Availability	Prompt injection, data and model poisoning, model theft, sensitive output disclosure, excessive agency, denial-of-wallet (see Chapter 2 and Chapter 7).
OT and IoT Compromise	Endpoint / OT	Availability, Integrity	Compromise of industrial control systems, medical devices, or connected fleets with physical-world consequences.
Physical Security Breach	Endpoint / OT / Data	Confidentiality, Availability	Unauthorized physical access to facilities, hardware theft, rogue devices, or tampering with on-site infrastructure.

This broader mapping also clarifies why different organizations set different priorities. A company that depends on customer trust and regulatory compliance will place heavy weight on confidentiality and privacy, pushing investment into email protection, identity governance, data classification, and privacy-aware monitoring. A company where downtime drives immediate revenue loss will place heavy weight on availability, pushing investment into resilience, segmentation, DDoS mitigation, and backup testing. Organizations that operate physical infrastructure will place additional weight on OT security and authenticity, because integrity failures there can create safety consequences that no pure IT incident can produce.

Risk = Likelihood × Impact, and Practical Risk Frameworks

Risk can be framed through a straightforward formula: risk equals likelihood multiplied by impact. The formula supports prioritization across threats that differ in frequency and severity, and it is the starting point for the risk frameworks leaders encounter most often.

NIST Cybersecurity Framework (CSF) 2.0 organizes security activities into six functions—Govern, Identify, Protect, Detect, Respond, Recover—that together cover the lifecycle of risk management. It does not prescribe controls; it gives leaders a structure to reason about coverage and maturity.

ISO/IEC 27001 and 27002 provide a certifiable information security management system with a detailed control catalog. Organizations pursuing formal attestation tend to align here.

FAIR (Factor Analysis of Information Risk) translates risk into quantitative terms—probable frequency and probable magnitude in monetary units—which helps when security priorities need to be compared against other business investments.

STRIDE and DREAD are threat-modeling frameworks that surface during design reviews. STRIDE categorizes threats (Spoofing, Tampering, Repudiation, Information disclosure, Denial of service, Elevation of privilege) and maps each to design mitigations. DREAD, less rigorously, scores severity dimensions.

AI changes both sides of the risk equation when used well. It reduces the likelihood by detecting threats earlier and strengthening prevention through anomaly-driven controls. It reduces impact by shrinking response and containment time, limiting blast radius, and reducing the chance that a foothold becomes a widespread compromise.

A practical approach for executives is to rate a small set of scenarios on both likelihood and impact, then align controls to the top of the list. If credential theft feels frequent and the impact includes access to customer records, prioritize phishing resistance, MFA coverage, and identity analytics. If ransomware impact is existential due to downtime, prioritize segmentation, backup testing, and rapid isolation steps. AI then supports these priorities by surfacing early indicators, ranking work, and shortening investigation time, while the chosen controls define what "good" looks like.

Caution matters too. AI programs can introduce operational risk when baselines are unstable, training data lacks coverage, or models drift. False positives create fatigue; false negatives create blind spots. Treat evaluation and governance as ongoing work, not a one-time rollout task.

Why the Baseline Still Decides Outcomes

AI performs best when the security baseline is strong and the operating environment is well managed. The baseline controls that enable reliable AI outcomes are familiar: strong authentication with phishing-resistant MFA, prompt patching, encrypted and tested backups, asset inventory with clear ownership, segmentation that limits lateral movement, and practiced incident response plans. This baseline also improves AI performance directly—by stabilizing "normal" behavior, which helps anomaly detection separate real issues from routine noise.

Leaders gain speed and clarity when they treat baseline maturity as part of AI adoption, rather than as a separate track. Asset visibility, identity discipline, patch consistency, segmentation hygiene, and tested recovery set the conditions for AI systems to deliver high-confidence detection and safe automation. A concrete pattern repeats: organizations that invested three to six months in baseline hardening before scaling AI detection report far fewer false positives, faster analyst adoption, and measurable drops in mean time to respond. Organizations that skipped that phase report the opposite.

Mapping a Ransomware Attack Across the CIA Triad

Ransomware provides a clear example of how CIA maps to business impact and how AI changes outcomes by compressing time.

In a traditional scenario, ransomware is detected late, many files are already encrypted, and teams rely heavily on backups and manual recovery. Availability takes the direct hit through outages and operational disruption. Integrity takes a hit as systems are corrupted and configurations are altered during the intrusion. Confidentiality takes a hit when attackers exfiltrate data before encryption and then apply extortion pressure over its potential release. Privacy impact often follows when regulated data is among the exfiltrated records. Authenticity failures can appear during the attack itself—a forged help-desk message, a deepfake approval—that unlocked the initial foothold.

In an AI-enhanced scenario, the sequence looks different. AI detects abnormal file-encryption behavior early and isolates the impacted server automatically. The system correlates rapid file access patterns with suspicious PowerShell execution and an administrator login from a new location. A consolidated alert reaches the SOC with clear evidence. An account lockout is triggered. The team restores affected files and keeps core operations running. Only a small portion of files are affected, downtime stays minimal, and telemetry indicates no meaningful data exfiltration.

The difference is not magic. It is the combination of disciplined fundamentals—segmentation, least privilege, asset inventory, tested backups, monitored privileged accounts—with AI correlation across layers. Remove the fundamentals, and the AI still fires alerts, but the containment either never happens or happens too late. This is the single most important pattern in the chapter.

Attack Vectors vs AI-Enhanced Defenses

A threat-to-defense view helps leaders place AI in the right spots and keep expectations grounded. The table below pairs each vector with the traditional controls that must still be in place and the AI enhancements that add speed and context.

Table 3.2: Each vector requires both a disciplined baseline and AI enhancement. AI without the baseline produces noise; the baseline without AI cannot keep up with attacker scale.

Attack Vector	Traditional Defense (Baseline)	AI-Enhanced Defense
Phishing and BEC	Spam filtering, user training, MFA	NLP-based content analysis, sender-behavior modeling, deepfake detection, context-aware risk scoring
Credential Abuse	MFA, session controls, least privilege	UEBA, adaptive authentication, session anomaly detection, token-misuse analytics
Unpatched Vulnerabilities	Patch management, vulnerability scanning, WAF	Exploit-likelihood prioritization, reachability analysis, behavior-based exploit detection
Cloud Misconfiguration	CSPM, IaC policy checks, least-privilege review	AI-ranked posture findings, runtime correlation with control-plane events, drift, and anomaly detection
API Abuse	Authentication, rate limiting, schema validation	Behavior modeling per API, business-logic anomaly detection, credential misuse correlation
Ransomware	EDR, segmentation, immutable backups	Real-time encryption-pattern detection, cross-layer correlation, auto-isolation with human-in-the-loop
Data Exposure / Shadow AI	DLP, classification, access controls	Unstructured-data classification, egress anomaly detection, AI-tool traffic analytics
Insider Threat	Access reviews, DLP, audit logging	UEBA, off-hours access and exfiltration pattern detection, peer-group comparison
Supply Chain	Vendor assessments, SBOM, code review	Dependency risk scoring, behavior monitoring of third-party components, model and dataset provenance checks
DDoS	Scrubbing, rate limiting, CDN	ML traffic classification, early precursor detection, adaptive mitigation
AI-Specific Attacks	Input validation, sandboxing, least-privilege tools	Prompt injection filters, output classifiers, agent telemetry analytics, red-teaming cadence (Chapter 2)

Attack Vector	Traditional Defense (Baseline)	AI-Enhanced Defense
OT and IoT	Network segmentation, device hardening, monitoring	Behavior modeling on OT protocols, multimodal correlation of cyber and physical signals
Physical Security	Access control, CCTV, tamper detection	Video analytics, behavior anomaly detection, correlation with identity and badge-reader events

This table clarifies where AI provides a unique advantage. AI excels at pattern recognition, anomaly detection, correlation, and prioritization. Traditional controls provide deterministic enforcement, baseline prevention, and resilience scaffolding. Programs succeed when both operate together, with clear handoffs between prevention, detection, and response.

Case Study: NotPetya, Maersk, and the Cost of Weak Fundamentals

NotPetya remains one of the clearest reminders of what large-scale availability failure looks like. In 2017, NotPetya operated as a wiper masquerading as ransomware, causing massive data destruction and spreading globally through a compromised software update—a textbook supply-chain attack. Many organizations saw systems rendered unrecoverable and operations halted. Companies with strong availability planning, including offline backups and well-practiced recovery, recovered faster and with less long-term damage.

The Maersk recovery story is widely referenced for a reason. The company rebuilt its network using a single surviving domain controller located in an office in Ghana that happened to be offline during the attack. That detail captures a resilience lesson that no amount of AI can substitute for: offline integrity copies and recovery processes can determine whether an enterprise can rebuild trust in its core identity systems after catastrophic disruption. Estimated losses across Maersk and other affected companies ran into billions of dollars, much of it driven by extended operational downtime rather than by the initial compromise.

NotPetya also reinforces the value of basic practices that scale across any security stack and against any attack vector. Network segmentation limits the spread by preventing malware from moving freely across the environment. Least privilege reduces reach by limiting what compromised accounts can access. Offline or immutable backups provide a recovery path when systems become unrecoverable through any mechanism—ransomware, wiper, insider action, accidental deletion, cloud-account compromise. Tested restore procedures turn backups from a checkbox into a capability.

AI would have changed the detection and containment timeline materially in an organization hit by NotPetya—unusual lateral movement, destructive behavior patterns, and privileged account misuse are exactly the signals AI correlation is strong at. But the case still shows that backups, segmentation, and least privilege decide long-term survival once destructive malware takes hold. Fundamentals are what allowed the organizations that recovered to recover at all.

KPIs to Track

Fundamentals improve when leaders measure them consistently, assign ownership, and review them with the same discipline used for other operational metrics. A review rhythm helps—weekly operational checks for patch and phishing metrics, monthly for restore readiness and configuration drift, quarterly for the metrics that connect to risk posture and investment priorities.

Patch compliance. Track the percentage of critical systems patched within policy timeframes and aim above 90%. If AI supports prioritization, track the reduction in days to patch high-risk exploitable vulnerabilities. A move from a 45-day median patch time to 14 days on reachable critical vulnerabilities is a recognizable milestone.

Phishing success rate. From periodic exercises, track click-through and credential submission rates. When AI email defenses are introduced, expect a measurable decline across subsequent campaigns—simulated click-through moving from 18% to below 6% within two quarters is typical for programs that invest in both tooling and training.

Cloud posture score. Track the percentage of cloud resources compliant with hardened baselines, segmented by criticality, and trend it. A quarterly improvement of 10% starting from a 60% baseline is a meaningful trajectory.

Identity hygiene. Track MFA coverage on privileged and critical accounts (target 100%), percentage of dormant accounts deactivated, and time to revoke access after role change or termination. Non-human identities—service accounts, CI/CD tokens, AI agent credentials—deserve the same tracking.

Data classification coverage. Track the percentage of critical data stores with proper classification and encryption. AI can help identify shadow IT repositories and unknown data stores; low coverage signals a need to improve visibility before relying heavily on AI analytics that may miss unknown data paths.

Backup and restore readiness. Regularly test backups and track the time to restore critical systems alongside the success rate of test restores. "Backups we test monthly" is a different control from "backups we have," and only the first survives a NotPetya-class event.

MTTR by attack type. Break down mean time to recover by categories—phishing, ransomware, cloud misconfiguration exploitation, identity compromise, AI-specific incidents. Segmentation reveals where fundamentals are weak and where AI assistance will help most.

Risks and Guardrails

Strong fundamentals plus AI produce powerful outcomes, and the combination carries predictable risks leaders can manage through clear guardrails.

Fundamental neglect. Leaders sometimes assume monitoring reduces the need for routine controls. The guardrail keeps programs healthy: maintain audits and compliance checks for baseline controls, keep regular patching, access reviews, and backup drills on schedule, and treat AI alerts as an addition to those controls rather than a substitute.

Alert fatigue from weak baselines. When many systems are misconfigured, AI flags large volumes of issues, and teams stop paying attention. The guardrail is sequencing—clean up known issues first through hardening and patching, then rely more heavily on real-time AI monitoring once noise reduces. A short "phase zero" focused on baseline hygiene before scaling AI detection pays back quickly in trust and analyst throughput.

False sense of security. Leaders can overestimate AI's capabilities. Guardrails include leadership education on model limits, layered defenses that assume some threats pass through, and red-team drills that test whether AI systems detect simulated attacks—revealing blind spots in a controlled way before an adversary does.

Misalignment with risk appetite. AI can recommend controls that conflict with business reality—blocking access from a geography where operations exist, blocking a payment flow during a legitimate volume spike, isolating a production system during a promotion. The guardrail involves risk management in tuning AI policies, aligning thresholds to business needs, and encoding policy context so the system reflects acceptable activity.

Compliance backfire. Basic controls map directly to frameworks such as ISO 27001, NIST CSF, HIPAA, PCI DSS, and DPDPA. Leaders gain safety when they map AI-enhanced controls to these frameworks, continue manual controls where required, or obtain audit approval for AI-based controls with evidence that they work. Documentation matters when AI systems adjust configurations, because logs and evidence support compliance and protect the integrity of records. Teams gain extra safety by recording tuning decisions, escalation thresholds, and the rationale behind policy exceptions, so audits and incident reviews can trace who approved what and why.

Backup-as-theater. A backup that has never been restored is a belief, not a control. The guardrail is scheduled restore drills, with reporting on restore time and success rate, and the willingness to declare a backup strategy broken when drills fail.

Executive Takeaways

- **Secure the basics first, then amplify with AI.** Foundational hygiene decides whether AI produces clarity or noise. Invest in baseline maturity as part of AI adoption, not as a separate track.
- **Think CIA plus Privacy plus Authenticity.** The extended pillars give leaders the vocabulary to connect technical events to business consequences across modern incidents, including AI-specific and privacy-driven ones.
- **Adopt zero trust as the operating principle.** Implicit trust based on network location or prior access no longer scales across cloud, SaaS, remote work, and non-human identities, including AI agents.
- **Defense in depth remains the backbone.** Multiple overlapping controls mean no single failure becomes a compromise. AI correlates across layers at a speed humans cannot match—which is why the layers must be there in the first place.
- **Treat the full attack vector landscape as the scope.** Phishing, credentials, unpatched software, cloud misconfiguration, API abuse, ransomware, data exposure, insider threats, supply chain, DDoS, AI-specific attacks, OT/IoT, and physical—each needs explicit attention, with priorities set by your risk appetite and business reality.
- **Use risk frameworks to align, not just audit.** NIST CSF for structure, ISO 27001 for certification, FAIR for quantification, STRIDE for design—these are tools for leadership conversation, not just compliance artifacts.
- **Measure the fundamentals consistently.** Patch compliance, phishing resilience, cloud posture, identity hygiene, data classification, backup readiness, and MTTR by attack type are the honest signals. Review them on a cadence with clear ownership.
- **Resilience still decides survival.** NotPetya showed what catastrophic availability failure looks like. Segmentation, least privilege, offline backups, and tested restore procedures are what let organizations rebuild. No amount of AI replaces them.

End-of-Chapter Reflection Questions

- For each of the five pillars—confidentiality, integrity, availability, privacy, authenticity—can you name the top two controls currently protecting your organization, and the top two gaps?
- Which three attack vectors from the expanded landscape represent your highest exposure today, and does your current investment match that ranking?
- If your organization suffered a NotPetya-class event tomorrow, how long would full operational recovery take? When was that answer last tested rather than estimated?
- Where are implicit-trust assumptions still baked into your architecture, and what would a twelve-month zero-trust roadmap look like?
- For each risk framework your organization uses—NIST CSF, ISO 27001, FAIR, STRIDE, DPDPA, or local equivalent—is the output used for leadership decisions, or only for compliance artifacts?
- Which of your current AI-enhanced controls would still function effectively if the underlying baseline (patching, identity, segmentation) regressed by 20%? Which would collapse?
- If you drew the defense-in-depth stack for a specific crown-jewel system today, which layer would you find weakest, and what would closing that gap cost?
- When was the last full restore drill, and what was the gap between the documented recovery time objective and the actual time observed?

Part 2

AI IN ACTION (PRACTICAL SECURITY APPLICATIONS)

Chapter 4

AI-POWERED SECURE SOFTWARE DEVELOPMENT LIFECYCLE

The Speed Gap That Broke Traditional SSDLC

The Secure Software Development Lifecycle was designed for a pace that no longer exists. A decade ago, a typical enterprise team shipped a few releases a quarter. Security reviews ran in weeks. Penetration testing ran annually. Vulnerability management meant a monthly patch window. That rhythm fit the pace of the business, and the security team's calendar more or less lined up with the engineering team's calendar.

The modern reality is different in kind, not degree. Organizations that have adopted continuous delivery now ship hundreds or thousands of production changes a day. Infrastructure is defined as code and rebuilt from scratch with every commit. Dependencies update weekly, sometimes daily. AI coding assistants accelerate individual developer throughput by measurable multiples. The engineering calendar has compressed from months to hours, while the security calendar, in many organizations, has not compressed at all.

That gap is where incidents now live. Vulnerabilities reach production before the next quarterly review. Dependency updates introduce silent supply-chain compromises before anyone reads the changelog. Misconfigurations in infrastructure-as-code templates propagate across hundreds of workloads before the first alert fires. A CI/CD pipeline, holding production credentials and signing keys, becomes a target because every engineering team depends on it, and most security teams do not fully understand its trust boundaries.

AI is not an optional accelerator for SSDLC. It is the only way to close the speed gap. The proposition is straightforward: machine-speed analysis, prioritization, and remediation across every stage of the lifecycle, with humans retaining ownership of decisions that carry meaningful consequences. The risk, equally straightforward, is that the same AI that accelerates defense also accelerates failure modes—subtly vulnerable code shipped at scale, agents with excessive permissions acting autonomously in production, source code leaking through unsanctioned tooling. This chapter is about doing the first without triggering the second.

The SSDLC loop from Chapter 1—plan, build, test, deploy, run, observe, with feedback from observe back into plan and build—is the reference model. This chapter goes deep into every stage, with AI and governance treated as first-class citizens at each one.

The Modern Development Reality

Four forces have reshaped how modern software is built, and each one changes what security has to do.

Development velocity has compounded. High-performing engineering organizations deploy to production dozens or hundreds of times per day. The lead time from commit to production, once measured in weeks, now measures in minutes for many teams. A security model that relies on pre-deployment human review at every stage cannot keep up, and the teams that try it become the bottleneck the business works around.

AI coding assistants have moved from optional to pervasive. Cursor, Claude Code, GitHub Copilot, and autonomous coding agents such as Devin-class systems are now present in most professional development environments. Recent surveys suggest that a majority of professional developers use AI assistants daily, and a meaningful portion of committed code is AI-generated or AI-modified. This raises productivity and also raises the stakes on every downstream control, because the thing producing code now also produces vulnerabilities faster.

Software supply chains have become long and opaque. A typical application depends on hundreds of direct and thousands of transitive dependencies, each with its own maintainers, build systems, and attack surface. Well-known supply-chain incidents—SolarWinds, Codecov, dependency-confusion attacks, compromised GitHub Actions—showed that upstream compromise propagates to downstream consumers faster than detection usually moves.

The CI/CD pipeline has become critical infrastructure. Build systems, artifact registries, signing services, and deployment orchestrators collectively hold production credentials, cryptographic keys, and the ability to ship code directly to production. In many organizations, the pipeline has more privilege than any single human employee. That concentration of trust makes it a high-value target and a high-value control surface in equal measure.

Each of these forces has a natural AI response. Velocity is absorbed by AI-assisted review, prioritization, and auto-remediation. AI coding assistants are governed by sanctioned tooling, IP controls, and model-aware code review. Supply chains are analyzed for reachability, provenance, and behavior using AI. Pipelines are hardened through AI-driven posture analysis and continuous monitoring. The chapter works through each in turn.

Key Data Points and Supporting Evidence

Four patterns anchor the chapter.

Developers spend a large fraction of their time on security-adjacent work—when the tooling works. Surveys consistently show that developers, not security engineers, write the majority of fixes that reduce risk. The bottleneck is rarely developer willingness; it is signal quality, prioritization, and fix ergonomics. AI shifts each of these, which is why the productivity case and the security case reinforce each other.

Most security findings are false positives or not reachable in production. Traditional SAST and SCA tools produce thousands of findings, of which a small fraction are exploitable. Teams that drown in noise stop triaging. Teams that use AI for reachability analysis, exploit-likelihood scoring, and business-context prioritization consistently report two- to five-fold reductions in findings requiring human review without reducing real-risk coverage.

Supply-chain compromise has outpaced direct application exploitation in some sectors. Financial services, critical infrastructure, and software-as-a-service providers report a meaningful share of material incidents traced to third-party or fourth-party code, packages, models, or dataset compromises. Defensive investment in SBOM, provenance, and AI-driven dependency analysis has risen accordingly.

AI-assisted development measurably accelerates throughput, with mixed effects on defect rates. Published research on AI coding assistants shows productivity gains in the twenty-to-fifty percent range for many tasks, alongside evidence that AI-generated code, if ungoverned, can introduce subtle vulnerabilities at rates comparable to or higher than human-written code. The value extraction depends on review discipline, not on turning off the tool.

These patterns tell a single operational story: the modern SSDLC cannot rely on pre-deployment manual gates to catch everything, cannot rely on traditional signature-based scanning to cut through noise, and cannot leave AI coding tools ungoverned. The rest of this chapter details the alternative.

Insights and Practical Frameworks

The AI-Enhanced SSDLC: A Closer Look

Chapter 1 introduced the SSDLC loop at a high level. Chapter 4 goes deeper, placing concrete AI capabilities at every stage. The diagram below expands the original.

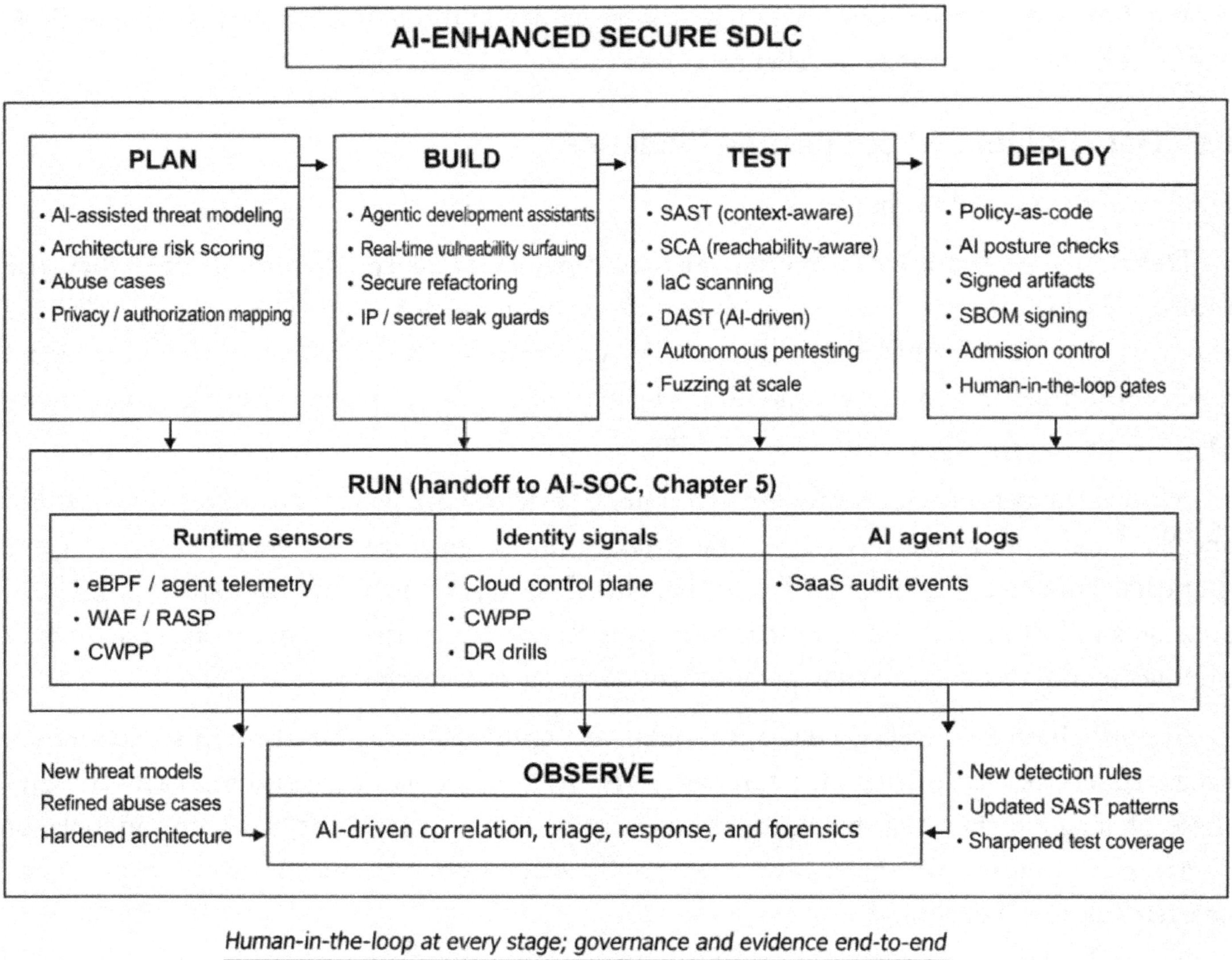

Figure 4.1: The AI-enhanced SSDLC. AI is present at every stage; runtime telemetry feeds back into plan and build; the SOC (Chapter 5) owns run and observe.

Two framing points matter as we work through the stages. First, AI is not a replacement for any existing stage—it is an amplifier at every stage. Removing SAST and replacing it with AI is not the point; making SAST accurate, contextual, and actionable using AI is the point. Second, the feedback loop from run and observe back into plan and build is what turns the SSDLC from a pipeline into a learning system. Incident patterns become new threat models. Production anomalies become new SAST rules. That loop is where the program compounds, or—if it is missing—where it stagnates.

Secure-by-Design with AI: Continuous Threat Modeling

Threat modeling has historically been a one-time activity at the start of a project, usually conducted in a whiteboard session and captured in a document that nobody updates. The design evolves, the threat model does not, and the gap between them becomes a source of missed controls and surprising incidents.

AI makes continuous threat modeling practical. Given an architecture description—from diagrams, infrastructure-as-code, or live system introspection—an AI can generate a STRIDE-aligned threat model, map threats to existing controls, identify coverage gaps, and re-run the analysis whenever the architecture changes. The output is not a replacement for human judgment. It is a draft that a senior engineer or security architect can refine in a fraction of the time a manual threat model takes.

Three practical patterns work well. Design-review copilots ingest a design document or architecture diagram and surface threat categories, trust boundaries, and suggested mitigations, leaving the final call to the reviewer. Architecture-as-code analysis continuously scans Terraform, CloudFormation, or Kubernetes manifests for deviations from secure patterns and surfaces the risk implications. Abuse-case generation asks the AI to produce misuse scenarios for a given user story, which frequently surfaces failure modes the happy-path design obscures.

The extended CIA pillars from Chapter 3 map directly into the threat-modeling output. For each new component, the reviewer should be able to answer: which pillar does this protect, which does it put at risk, and what control prevents the most likely failure mode? A design that cannot answer those three questions is not ready to build.

Agentic AI in the Development Phase

The largest productivity shift in software engineering in the past decade is the move from manually typed code to AI-assisted authoring. The practical security implications are material and are covered in three angles below.

Productivity, code quality, and security. AI coding assistants—Cursor, Claude Code, GitHub Copilot, and autonomous agents—help developers write code faster, explore unfamiliar codebases, and refactor at scale. In security terms, the same capability can also surface vulnerable patterns during authoring (missing input validation, weak cryptographic choices, hardcoded secrets, unsafe deserialization), recommend safer alternatives, and suggest fixes for flagged issues. Teams that integrate security-aware AI review into the IDE report faster defect-to-fix cycles and, over time, measurable shifts in the patterns developers write by default.

Shadow dev tools and IP leakage. The pattern from Chapter 1—engineers using unsanctioned consumer AI services to debug code, refactor, or explore solutions—is the single most common source of source-code exposure in most enterprises today. The mechanism is quiet: a developer pastes a proprietary algorithm or an internal API key into a consumer assistant to save an hour, and the snippet becomes part of an index, a training dataset (depending on terms), or a provider log with uncertain retention. No system was compromised. Intellectual property left anyway.

The fix is not a ban; bans fail because developers will route around them. The fix combines four elements: a sanctioned enterprise-tier AI coding assistant with contractual data protections, logging, and repository allow-lists; proxy-level visibility into AI service usage so shadow traffic is measurable; an updated acceptable-use policy and contributor/contractor agreements that explicitly cover AI-assisted development; and developer enablement that teaches the sanctioned workflow for the tasks people were trying to accelerate. Organizations that implement all four routinely see shadow AI traffic drop by eighty percent or more within a quarter.

The dual-use reality. The same agentic tools that accelerate shipping can ship vulnerable code faster. Research on AI-generated code has repeatedly found rates of insecure patterns—injection-vulnerable string construction, improperly handled credentials, broken authentication logic—that match or exceed human-written code when AI suggestions are accepted uncritically. Productivity gains do not automatically become security gains. They become security gains when the same AI stack that writes code also reviews it, the same enterprise tier that logs prompts also flags secrets in context, and the same PR process that accepted "accept suggestion" also requires reviewer sign-off for security-sensitive paths. Treating AI-generated code as trusted because a human clicked accept is a recipe for fast-scaling defects; treating it as untrusted until reviewed is the operating discipline that extracts the value.

AI-Driven CI/CD Pipeline Security

CI/CD pipelines are where the security posture of everything else gets assembled. A vulnerability caught at the pipeline stage costs hours to fix. The same vulnerability missed at the pipeline stage and surfaced in production costs days or weeks and often involves customer impact.

Pipeline posture and policy-as-code. AI strengthens pipeline security by continuously evaluating pipeline configurations—who can trigger what, which secrets are available to which jobs, which artifacts can be signed and by whom, which deployments require approval—and surfacing drift from secure baselines. Policy-as-code tools like Open Policy Agent and Kyverno provide the enforcement layer; AI provides the prioritization, the explanation, and the risk-based approval logic that makes policy changes defensible to engineering teams.

Risk-based build approval is one of the most practical applications. For a low-risk change—a documentation update, a dependency patch that passes all tests and reachability checks—the pipeline promotes through to production automatically. For a change that touches authentication code, modifies an IAM policy, or introduces a new external dependency, the pipeline requires reviewer approval, with the AI providing the context the reviewer needs to decide in minutes rather than hours. This is the HITL tiering from Chapter 1 applied to the build system.

The pipeline itself as an attack surface. A modern CI/CD pipeline holds production deployment credentials, code-signing keys, cloud provider tokens, container registry credentials, and often direct access to the most sensitive datastores. An attacker who compromises a pipeline compromises everything downstream, often without tripping any application-layer defense.

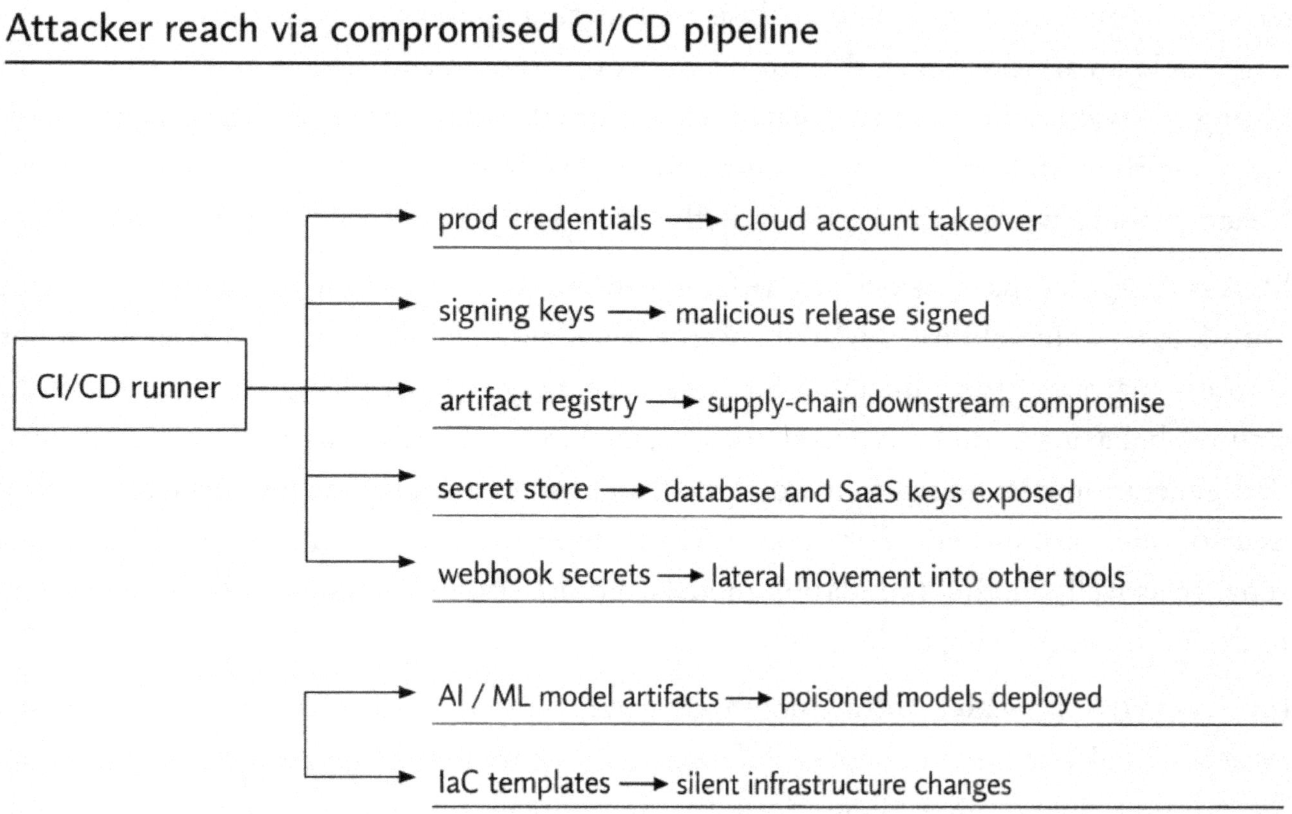

Figure 4.2: A compromised CI/CD pipeline gives an attacker broad reach. Pipeline hardening is not optional.

Defensive patterns follow directly from the reach. Scope credentials per job rather than per pipeline, with short-lived tokens preferred over long-lived keys. Use signed, versioned, attested build artifacts so a compromised runner cannot inject unsigned content downstream. Separate build and deploy phases, with deployment using tokens the build phase never sees. Maintain an inventory of every action, extension, and third-party integration the pipeline invokes, and treat that inventory with the same discipline as an application SBOM. Log every pipeline event as security telemetry and feed it into the SOC (Chapter 5). AI assists here by spotting anomalous pipeline activity—unusual job sequences, unexpected credential use, new integrations—that a human review cadence cannot catch in real time.

AI-Enhanced Security Testing

Security testing produced most of the noise that originally broke the SSDLC. Teams had tools, the tools prduced findings, findings piled up, and engineering learned to ignore them. AI changes the economics of testing by making each category of tool contextual, prioritized, and actionable.

SAST with context and exploitability. Static Application Security Testing has long been accurate at finding patterns and poor at judging which ones matter. AI-enhanced SAST combines pattern detection with reachability analysis (is this code path actually invoked?), exploitability scoring (could an attacker reach this from a network-exposed endpoint?), and business-context weighting (does this code touch regulated data or privileged operations?). The practical effect is the same ten thousand raw findings reduced to the two hundred that warrant human attention, with each of those two hundred arriving with a clear rationale.

SCA and supply-chain risk. Software Composition Analysis catalogs dependencies and maps them to known vulnerabilities. AI enhancement adds reachability—the CVE in an imported library only matters if the vulnerable function is actually called—plus provenance verification, maintainer-behavior signals, typosquatting detection, and malicious-package identification. SBOM generation becomes automatic, signed, and versioned. Dependency updates are ranked by security value, not just age. For agentic AI development, SCA extends to model and dataset provenance as well, treating foundation models and fine-tuning datasets with the same supply-chain discipline as code dependencies.

IaC security at scale. Infrastructure-as-code templates—Terraform, CloudFormation, Kubernetes manifests, Helm charts—define cloud posture before anything runs. AI-enhanced IaC scanning catches misconfigurations (public storage, over-privileged roles, unencrypted databases, open security groups) at commit time, explains the business impact, and generates the compliant version of the template as a suggested diff. At scale, this is the single most efficient place to improve cloud security; a single IaC pattern fix can prevent hundreds of production misconfigurations over a year.

AI-assisted DAST. Dynamic Application Security Testing runs against running applications. AI enhancement contributes in three ways. Test generation becomes smarter—the AI proposes test inputs that exercise edge cases and likely-vulnerable code paths rather than brute-forcing parameter space. Authentication and session handling are managed intelligently across multi-step flows, which is where classical DAST often breaks. Findings are triaged and deduplicated before they reach the engineering queue.

Autonomous and continuous pentesting (defender view). Autonomous pentesting platforms run continuously or on-cadence against production-representative environments, chaining vulnerabilities the way a human adversary would. From the defender's adoption perspective, three questions decide value. First, scope: what systems are in-scope, what data are off-limits, and how are destructive actions prevented? Second, oversight: who reviews findings before remediation effort is spent, and how are false positives retired? Third, integration: do findings flow into the same prioritization and remediation path as SAST and SCA findings, or do they live in a separate queue that nobody reads? Organizations that adopt autonomous pentesting and answer these three questions up front tend to extract value. Organizations that adopt it as a marketing checkbox tend to generate shelfware. Chapter 2's AI red-teaming framework applies here—pre-launch gate for high-risk deployments, cadence post-launch, findings that drive model, controls, and detection changes together.

AI-Led Remediation and Validation

Finding defects is half the work. Fixing them is the other half, and the place where most security programs lose their engineering partners.

Contextual fix recommendations. AI-led remediation moves beyond "here is a defect" to "here is a defect, here is the specific fix appropriate for this codebase's conventions, here are the tests that would validate it, here is the pull request." The transition from finding to fix, historically measured in days or weeks because a developer had to context-switch into a security task, collapses into minutes. Engineering teams treat AI-remediated findings very differently from raw scanner findings because the cognitive cost to act has dropped.

Auto-generated PRs with HITL tiering. Not every auto-PR is safe to merge automatically. Chapter 1's HITL framework applies directly. The tiering that works in practice:

Fully automated (human-out). Dependency bumps to patched versions with passing tests, IaC template fixes with policy-as-code verification, and auto-formatting of already-approved security fixes. These land without human review because they are mechanical, reversible, and well-understood.

Human-on-the-loop. Input validation fixes, logging additions, straightforward authorization checks. The AI generates the PR; a reviewer approves; the AI handles the mechanics of merging and rolling back if tests fail. The human is in the critical path, but the cognitive burden is minimal.

Human-in-the-loop (required). Changes to authentication logic, cryptographic primitives, IAM policies, data-handling code subject to privacy regulation, business-logic changes that could affect availability. The AI proposes; a qualified reviewer approves before anything merges. There is no fast path here, by design.

The tiering needs to be explicit in the pipeline configuration, reviewed quarterly, and expanded or narrowed based on incident data. Organizations that document the tiering and tune it as trust accumulates avoid both ends of the failure mode—too much automation causing production incidents, too little causing the program to stall.

Continuous revalidation. Fixing a defect is necessary but not sufficient. The same vulnerability can be reintroduced a week later by a different developer, a merged branch, a dependency update, or a rollback that accidentally brings back old code. Continuous revalidation means the AI tracks not just open findings but the patterns that produced them, and re-tests every time the codebase changes. A regression in a previously fixed vulnerability should generate a higher-priority alert than a new finding, because regression indicates that a control is not holding.

Build-Deploy-Run: Closing the Lifecycle

SSDLC does not stop at deploy. The code that reaches production enters the phase where most of the real-world testing happens, against actual adversaries, under actual load, with actual consequences. Three operational concerns belong inside SSDLC even though they are often treated as separate.

Availability and resilience as security controls. Availability is a CIA pillar, not an afterthought. A deployment pipeline that reliably ships fast is only useful if it can also reliably roll back fast. A system designed to auto-scale is only resilient if the scaling decisions remain intact when the control plane is under attack. AI contributes by continuously evaluating resilience properties—failover readiness, auto-scaling behavior, circuit-breaker configurations—and flagging when a production change has weakened them, even if the change passed all other checks.

Backup and disaster-recovery security. Backups that have never been restored are belief, not control (Chapter 3). Backups themselves are increasingly an attack target—ransomware operators now routinely attempt to destroy or encrypt backups before the main encryption phase, to prevent recovery. Secure backup posture means immutable storage, offline copies, signed and integrity-verified restore paths, and regularly tested recovery procedures. AI contributes to backup security by detecting anomalies in backup job patterns, flagging unusual access to backup systems, and correlating backup anomalies with other intrusion signals (which, in a compromise, often precede destructive actions by hours or days).

Secure runtime posture. The deployed application is a living system. Runtime application self-protection, runtime container security, eBPF-based process observation, and cloud workload protection together give the SSDLC its runtime feedback loop. AI correlates these runtime signals with build-time knowledge—the SBOM, the threat model, the detected-but-accepted risks—so runtime detection becomes sharper. A vulnerability marked as "not reachable" during build-time SAST gets a different alert weighting if runtime telemetry shows the vulnerable function is now being called.

This is the bridge to Chapter 5. Runtime sensors, observability, incident detection, investigation, and response are the domain of the AI-SOC. The feedback from the SOC—what was detected, what was missed, what patterns keep recurring—flows back into SSDLC as new threat models, new SAST patterns, new SCA signatures, new pipeline gates. The loop closes. The program compounds.

Case Studies

Case Study 1: Agentic Dev Adoption at a FinTech

A mid-sized fintech with roughly four hundred engineers faced two simultaneous pressures. Product leadership wanted every team using AI coding assistants by the end of the year to hold velocity against larger competitors. The CISO had spent the previous quarter investigating two shadow AI incidents—one in which an engineer had pasted customer data extraction logic into a consumer assistant, and one in which a contractor had been using a browser-based coding tool that indexed repository snippets to improve suggestions.

The response ran three workstreams in parallel. An enterprise-tier AI coding assistant was procured with contractual zero-retention, single-tenant processing, and integration with the corporate identity provider, so usage was attributable. The deployment included repository allow-lists (internal-only repositories could not be indexed by the assistant's suggestion features), secret-scanning in the prompt path so hardcoded credentials were flagged before leaving the IDE, and logging that fed into the SOC as a new telemetry source.

In parallel, the security team published an acceptable-use policy specifically for AI-assisted development. It named the sanctioned tool, prohibited the consumer tools that had produced the incidents, and updated employment and contractor agreements to cover AI-assisted development explicitly, aligned with the firm's existing obligations under local privacy law and emerging AI regulation. The policy was paired with a thirty-minute enablement session covering what the sanctioned tool could do for each of the top five tasks the engineers had been using consumer tools for.

The third workstream was measurement. The proxy tracked unsanctioned AI traffic from engineering endpoints. The sanctioned tool reported utilization by team. The SOC added detections for secret exfiltration via AI services. And a quarterly review tracked not just adoption but incidents, time-to-fix on security findings, and developer satisfaction with the change.

Six months in, the metrics told a coherent story. Unsanctioned AI traffic from engineering had dropped by roughly ninety-two percent. The sanctioned tool had reached eighty-three percent adoption. Time-to-fix on critical SAST findings dropped from a median of eleven days to under three, because the AI surfaced the fix alongside the finding. Secret-leak incidents dropped to zero over the measurement period. Developer NPS on the AI tooling exceeded that of the internal build system. The CISO described the outcome as the single highest-leverage investment the security team had made in the past two years—not because the AI itself was extraordinary, but because the governance, enablement, and measurement around it were disciplined.

The lesson is the one Chapter 1 seeded, and this chapter reinforces: agentic AI in development is a governance problem that looks like a tooling problem. The tool is the easy part. Sanctioned alternatives, contractual protections, observability, and developer enablement are what turn it from a risk into a capability.

Case Study 2: Preventing a CI/CD Supply-Chain Compromise

A software-as-a-service company serving enterprise customers discovered, during a routine AI-driven pipeline posture review, that one of its GitHub Actions workflows had been updated two weeks earlier to reference a third-party action at a newly published version. The action itself had a credible maintainer and had been in use at the previous version for over a year. The new version had been released three weeks after a silent ownership transfer of the repository to an account with no prior history.

The AI posture tool flagged the change for three compounding reasons. The ownership-transfer pattern matched a historical template for supply-chain compromise. The new version introduced network calls to an endpoint that had not appeared in prior versions. And the action was invoked by a workflow that had access to the deployment pipeline's production credentials.

A human reviewer confirmed the flag in under an hour. The workflow was immediately pinned to the previous known-good commit hash, the third-party action was added to a block list, and an incident ticket was opened to review every dependency pinning policy in the organization. Further analysis of the suspicious version confirmed that it attempted to exfiltrate environment variables during execution, which in this organization's pipeline would have included production AWS credentials and a code-signing key.

The cost avoided was material. Exfiltration of the signing key would have allowed the attacker to produce signed malicious releases that downstream customers would have trusted. The public disclosure would have damaged the company's reputation with enterprise customers. The regulatory reporting obligations under customer contracts would have triggered weeks of response work. The actual cost, because the compromise was caught before execution, was a single afternoon of incident review and a one-week project to pin all third-party actions to commit hashes rather than version tags.

Three elements made the save possible. Continuous AI posture analysis of the pipeline, not episodic manual review. A risk-scoring model that flagged ownership-transfer and behavioral-change patterns together, not just known-bad indicators. And a human reviewer with the context to act quickly. None of the three was sufficient alone; all three together turned a potential supply-chain compromise into an uneventful afternoon.

The lesson is that the CI/CD pipeline is now a security surface that demands continuous AI attention. The attack patterns against it have matured. Manual review cadences, even rigorous ones, cannot keep up with the pace of third-party dependency change. AI in the pipeline is not a productivity feature; it is the control that holds the line.

KPIs to Track

KPIs for AI-SSDLC work when they connect security outcomes to engineering reality.

Time-to-fix on critical findings by severity. Track median and ninetieth-percentile time from finding to merged fix, segmented by severity and by source (SAST, SCA, IaC, DAST, runtime). A move from eleven days to three on critical SAST findings is a recognizable outcome of AI-led remediation.

Findings suppressed by AI triage versus findings surfaced to humans. Ratio matters more than absolute numbers. A program that suppresses ninety-five percent of raw findings with no increase in missed incidents is extracting real value. A program that suppresses ninety-five percent but sees incidents in the suppressed categories has miscalibrated and needs review.

Deployment frequency and lead time for changes, security-segmented. Track DORA-style deployment metrics alongside the percentage of deployments passing security gates. The goal is that security keeps pace with, and ultimately enables, engineering velocity—not that security slows it down.

Pipeline posture score. Track the percentage of pipelines compliant with hardened baselines: scoped credentials, signed artifacts, pinned actions, SBOM generation, and separation of build and deploy. Trend quarterly; target continuous improvement against a defined reference.

Shadow dev AI exposure. Measure unsanctioned AI service usage from engineering endpoints at the proxy. A program that can measure this is in a materially better position than one that cannot; a program with a trendline moving down from a known baseline is doing real work.

Coverage of crown-jewel systems by AI-assisted review. Track the percentage of services classified as crown-jewel that have AI-assisted SAST, SCA, IaC, and threat modeling enabled. Seventy percent is a milestone; forty percent is a gap worth naming.

Regression rate on previously fixed vulnerabilities. Track how often a vulnerability previously closed gets reintroduced within ninety days. High regression rates indicate that fixes did not propagate to developer behavior or that the continuous revalidation loop is not working.

Mean time to remediate supply-chain advisories. From CVE publication on a used dependency to a merged update across affected services. Under seventy-two hours on critical advisories is achievable with AI-assisted SCA and auto-PR on dependency bumps.

Risks and Guardrails

AI-SSDLC produces powerful outcomes and introduces specific failure modes. Guardrails keep the program credible.

Cavalier auto-remediation. An AI auto-PR that merges a subtly broken fix into production authentication code is an incident, not a win. The guardrail is the HITL tiering described earlier, enforced in the pipeline configuration and reviewed quarterly. Automation earns scope over time through demonstrated reliability; it does not start at maximum.

Unreviewed AI-generated code at scale. Treating AI suggestions as trusted because a developer clicked accept is the fast path to shipping vulnerabilities at velocity. The guardrail is the same code-review discipline that applies to human-written code, with specific attention to security-sensitive paths, combined with AI-assisted review running against AI-generated code before merge.

Shadow AI dev tools. Covered above. The guardrail stack is sanctioned tier, proxy visibility, policy, and enablement.

Supply-chain blind spots. An SBOM that covers direct dependencies but not transitive ones, or that covers code dependencies but not models and datasets, is giving false confidence. The guardrail is AI-assisted SCA with full transitive depth, model, and dataset provenance alongside code, and continuous verification against new advisories.

Pipeline trust creep. Over time, pipelines accumulate third-party actions, extensions, and integrations. Each is a potential supply-chain entry point. The guardrail is an inventory reviewed quarterly, pinning to commit hashes, not version tags, and AI-driven behavioral monitoring that flags new or changed dependencies for review.

Misaligned incentives. If engineering is measured purely on velocity and security on defect reduction, the two teams will push in opposite directions. The guardrail is shared metrics—deployment frequency with security gates passing, time-to-fix alongside deployment lead time, incidents alongside feature throughput—so both organizations optimize the same curve.

Over-reliance on AI code review. AI code review catches many patterns and misses some. The guardrail is defense in depth: AI review, human review, runtime detection, and incident response all catching different failures. A program that treats AI code review as the last line has moved the goalposts in the wrong direction.

Evidence and audit. Regulators, customers, and internal auditors increasingly ask which AI systems influenced which security decisions, and on what basis. The guardrail is logging that is automatic, durable, and queryable—every AI-assisted finding, every auto-PR, every suppressed alert, every threat-model draft. Reconstruction after the fact is too slow when audit pressure is real.

Executive Takeaways

- **The speed gap is structural.** Development velocity has compounded and will keep compounding. AI at every stage of SSDLC is not optional; it is the only way the security calendar keeps pace with the engineering calendar.
- **Agentic AI in development is a governance problem first.** Sanctioned tooling, contractual data protections, proxy visibility, and developer enablement matter more than the choice of tool. Bans fail; governance scales.
- **Treat AI-generated code as untrusted until reviewed.** The productivity gains are real; the security gains are conditional on review discipline. Clicking accept is not a security signal.
- **The CI/CD pipeline is critical infrastructure.** It holds production credentials, signing keys, and deployment power. Treat it as a security surface, not a developer convenience.
- **AI-enhanced testing is about signal, not volume.** SAST, SCA, IaC, DAST, and autonomous pen testing each produce actionable work only when AI adds reachability, exploitability, and business context. Without that, tools produce shelfware.
- **Auto-remediation needs Human in the loop (HITL) tiering, explicitly.** Fully automated for mechanical fixes, human-on-the-loop for routine fixes, human-in-the-loop for authentication, crypto, IAM, and privacy-sensitive code. Document the tiering; expand it as trust accumulates.

- **SSDLC includes running systems.** Availability, backup integrity, and runtime posture belong in the same lifecycle as build and test. The handoff to the AI-SOC (Chapter 5) is continuous, not a boundary.
- **The closed loop is where the program compounds.** Incidents feed threat models. Runtime findings sharpen SAST. Production telemetry informs build-time priorities. A program without that feedback stalls, regardless of tool quality.

End-of-Chapter Reflection Questions

- For your highest-traffic deployment pipeline, list every third-party action, extension, and integration it invokes. Which are pinned to commit hashes, and which to version tags? Which has been reviewed in the last ninety days?
- If an engineer wants to use an AI coding assistant today, what is the sanctioned path? Is it faster than the shadow path, or is the shadow path faster?
- Map each stage of your SSDLC to the AI capabilities in Figure 4.1. Which stages have AI coverage, which have gaps, and what is the plan for the gaps over the next two quarters?
- For auto-remediation in your pipelines today, where does human-in-the-loop start and end? Is that boundary documented, reviewed, and tuned—or implicit?
- When was the last time a vulnerability previously closed was reintroduced into your codebase? What process caught it, and how fast?
- If an attacker compromised your CI/CD pipeline this afternoon, what would they reach, and how long would it take you to know? Who owns that answer?
- For each of SAST, SCA, IaC, DAST, and pen testing, what percentage of findings today reach a developer's queue with the suggested fix attached? What would it take to raise that number?
- How does a finding from your AI-SOC turn into an updated SAST rule, a new threat model entry, or a sharpened pipeline gate? Is that loop instrumented, or aspirational?

Chapter 5

AI-POWERED SECURITY OPERATIONS CENTER

When Every Minute Starts Costing You

A security incident rarely arrives with a neat label. It arrives as messy signals—a few confused alerts, a user saying their laptop feels slow, an admin noticing a strange login, a service owner asking why a database has begun behaving oddly. In that moment, the team has two jobs running in parallel: stop the bleeding quickly and understand what happened well enough to prevent a repeat.

Traditional SOCs were built for a version of this job that no longer matches reality. Rule-based correlation, static thresholds, and manual triage worked when event volumes were lower, attack patterns were noisier, and environments were more contained. Today, the telemetry arrives from endpoints, cloud control planes, identity providers, SaaS applications, container orchestrators, CI/CD pipelines, and AI agents. The volume exceeds what any human team can process in real time, and the signals that matter most are often quiet—a credential used from a new ASN, a slight increase in database read loads, a cloud role modified at an unusual hour. Each one looks like noise alone. Together, they describe an intrusion.

The AI-powered SOC exists because this math does not resolve without machines. AI absorbs the volume, correlates the signals, prioritizes the queue, assists the investigation, and—within governed boundaries—executes response actions that would otherwise wait for a human who is already busy. The human role shifts from assembly-line triage to decision-making, judgment, and oversight. The combination is what lets a small team protect a large estate at the speed the adversary actually moves.

This chapter covers the full arc of that transformation: detection and prevention, agentic AI for SOC operations, incident response automation, digital forensics, and the closed feedback loop into the SSDLC from Chapter 4 that turns every incident into a defense improvement.

From Traditional SOC to AI-SOC

Three limits define the traditional SOC and explain why it has been overtaken.

Rule-based detection misses novel attacks. Signatures and correlation rules catch known patterns. They go silent when an attacker uses valid credentials, chains small steps across systems, or operates entirely inside authorized tools. The gap between known-pattern detection and the actual attack surface has widened every year, and it widened sharply when generative AI and agentic tools gave adversaries new ways to probe, impersonate, and automate.

Alert volume exceeds human capacity. A mid-sized SOC receiving two thousand alerts per day can spend its entire shift triaging, leaving little capacity for investigation, proactive hunting, or process improvement. When the majority of alerts are false positives or low value, the team learns to skim, and the incident that arrives as a quiet anomaly gets the same treatment as the noise around it.

Manual workflows create latency that the attacker exploits. Assembling a case from five different consoles, enriching it with identity and asset context, writing up the summary, escalating through the approval chain, and executing containment takes hours. In that window, the attacker moves laterally, elevates privileges, and stages exfiltration. The traditional SOC workflow and the attacker's operational tempo are no longer in the same time zone.

The AI-SOC addresses all three by introducing behavioral analytics for novel detection, machine-speed correlation and prioritization for volume, and orchestrated response automation for latency. The sections that follow go deeper into each.

Key Data Points and Supporting Evidence

Detection speed improves measurably. Organizations using AI-driven detection report reduced dwell times, with many moving from detection in days or weeks to detection in hours or less. Earlier detection limits privilege escalation, lateral movement, and data staging—and each of those reductions translates directly into lower breach cost.

Signal quality improves alongside speed. AI-based analytics routinely reduce false positive rates by roughly fifty percent and reduce alert triage time by comparable margins. When false positives fall, analysts spend more time on real cases, trust in the system rises, and investigation quality improves.

Containment accelerates. Automated IR platforms compress containment from days to hours or less. XYZ Bank (covered in the case studies below) moved the mean time to respond from roughly eight hours to under two hours after deploying AI-assisted automation.

The compounding effect is that faster containment also shortens investigation timelines, because the blast radius is smaller and the evidence set is more contained.

Root cause discovery becomes faster and more complete. AI stitches together attack timelines from scattered log sources in seconds rather than hours. This is not merely a speed gain—it is a quality gain, because under time pressure, human analysts frequently miss secondary persistence mechanisms, related credentials, or sibling compromises on adjacent systems.

The practical leadership test for an AI-SOC investment comes down to three questions: are we finding attacks earlier, can we handle the volume without burnout, and are we seeing fewer low-value alerts with better context attached? If the answer to all three is yes and the trend is improving, the program is working.

Insights and Practical Frameworks

AI-Driven Threat Detection and Prevention

AI-driven detection works across four complementary modes, each addressing a different part of the threat landscape.

Behavioral analytics and anomaly detection. The system learns what normal looks like for users, devices, services, and workloads, then flags deviations that carry risk. An insider accessing files at 3 AM with valid credentials triggers no signature rule. A behavioral model flags it because it deviates from the user's established pattern. This extends coverage into the "unknown" territory that rule-based systems cannot reach, including credential abuse, session hijacking, and privilege escalation using legitimate tools.

Cross-surface correlation. The six surfaces from Chapter 1—code, cloud, data, identity, endpoint, and OT, AI itself—each generate telemetry. AI's largest detection advantage is the ability to connect weak signals across those surfaces into coherent incident narratives. A suspicious email attachment, an unusual identity event, and a strange server process chain—each alone is noise; correlated, they describe a coordinated intrusion spanning initial access, identity targeting, and data staging. That correlation happens in seconds, and at a consistency humans cannot maintain at scale.

Predictive threat hunting. AI identifies patterns that precede attacks rather than only catching attacks in progress. A quiet server suddenly communicating frequently with a newly registered external domain may indicate reconnaissance or staging before a payload arrives. Vulnerability exploitation signals—exploit code publication, dark-web discussion, and active scanning—can be correlated to prioritize patching of the vulnerabilities which attackers are most likely to use first, turning patching from a backlog into a risk-driven queue.

Prevention through fast containment. When detection confidence is high and the action is bounded, AI can execute prevention in real time. Adaptive authentication that steps up when a login is anomalous. Automatic quarantine of an endpoint showing ransomware encryption behavior. Token revocation when a session anomaly exceeds a threshold. These are prevention actions, not just detections, and they follow the HITL tiering from Chapter 1: destructive or broad actions need human approval; narrow, reversible actions can run with supervision; high-confidence, low-blast-radius actions can execute fully automatically.

Agentic AI for SOC Operations

Agentic AI, defined in Chapter 2, moves from answering questions to taking actions. In the SOC, this means AI agents that investigate, enrich, pivot, and in some cases respond—autonomously executing multi-step workflows that previously required an analyst to sit across five consoles for forty minutes.

Autonomous investigation agents. An AI agent receives a high-priority alert. It queries the SIEM for related events in the surrounding time window. It enriches the source IP against threat intelligence. It pulls the affected user's recent authentication history from the identity provider. It checks whether the user's endpoint shows correlated process activity. It assembles the results into a case narrative and recommends next actions. The analyst opens the case and finds twenty minutes of investigative work already done, with citations and confidence levels attached to each finding.

MCP, non-human identity, and scope discipline. SOC agents connect to tools—SIEM, EDR, identity provider, cloud console, ticketing system—through MCP or equivalent integration protocols (Chapter 2). Each connection carries credentials and permissions. The governance principles that apply to any agent apply here: least-privilege tool access, scoped credentials with short lifetimes, logging of every tool call, and inventory of every MCP server the agent can reach. OWASP LLM06 (Excessive Agency) is directly relevant: a SOC agent that can query logs, revoke access, and modify firewall rules is an agent with a blast radius that exceeds its investigative purpose. Scope the agent to what it needs. Gate the rest behind human approval.

Security copilot as investigation accelerator. Language-based investigation assistants let analysts ask questions of logs in plain language and get correlated results in seconds. An analyst asks for unusual admin logins in the last twenty-four hours. The assistant responds with a specific admin login from a new IP in Romania at 3:47 AM, outside normal hours. The analyst asks for follow-up, and the assistant surfaces that the same account then accessed the finance database and ran a backup. The investigation that would have taken multiple manual queries across three tools is assembled in seconds. The analyst's time shifts from searching and formatting to validating and deciding.

AI-Assisted Incident Response

Incident response has a lifecycle: detect, triage, contain, investigate, remediate, recover, and learn. AI assists at every stage, and the real impact shows up in two places: time and consistency.

Intelligent triage: from alert flood to real incidents. During a serious incident, alerts multiply. Endpoint tools generate findings, identity systems show suspicious logins, and network tools show unusual traffic. AI clusters related alerts into incidents rather than presenting a pile of disjointed signals. An SOC that receives fifty isolated alerts can see those compressed into two incidents, with alerts grouped by campaign. A malware outbreak across ten endpoints gets split correctly: eight share the same strain (one response), two differ (separate response). That distinction can get lost when humans triage under time pressure.

Rapid root cause: timelines as a decision tool. AI stitches together the attack timeline from scattered signals in seconds: phishing email opened at 9:02, PowerShell executed at 9:05, lateral movement at 9:07, database access at 9:12. The timeline tells the team what to block (the domain), what to patch (the initial access vector), and what to verify (that no other accounts were compromised in the window). The timeline also functions as shared language among responders, IT owners, and executives, cutting hours back and forth.

Orchestrated containment with HITL tiering. When ransomware encryption begins, when credentials are being abused, or when a data breach is in motion, minutes matter. AI-driven automation can isolate hosts, kill processes, update firewall rules, revoke sessions, and reset credentials as soon as triggers fire. The HITL tiering from Chapter 1 keeps this safe. Fully automated: quarantine a single endpoint showing ransomware I/O patterns, block a known-malicious IP, and expire a leaked token. Human-on-the-loop: isolate a subnet, disable a non-privileged account, suspend a SaaS session. Human-in-the-loop required: isolate a domain controller, revoke privileged access at scale, lock an executive mailbox, block an entire cloud region. At 3 AM on a Sunday, automation executes the first tier the same way it would be at noon on a Tuesday. The consistency gain is as important as the speed gain.

Evidence preservation and sequencing. Containment actions can destroy volatile evidence—rebooting a machine clears memory where malware payloads, encryption keys, and lateral-movement artifacts lived. AI-guided sequencing captures memory snapshots and key logs before proceeding to containment. An evidence locker with chain-of-custody controls—timestamps, checksums, immutability—keeps evidence admissible and auditable for legal, regulatory, and post-incident learning.

AI as Collector, Connector, and Scribe. A helpful mental model for AI in IR: Collector gathers information fast from multiple sources. Connector links related evidence across systems into timelines. Scribe drafts the first version of the incident summary, affected-asset list, timeline narrative, and action checklist. The model keeps expectations grounded—AI helps the team move faster and stay consistent, and humans still decide what actions to take and what claims to make externally.

AI-Powered Forensics and Root Cause Analysis

Forensics requires discipline: preserve evidence, analyze artifacts, build a timeline, identify what was affected, and document findings. AI accelerates the analysis by scanning disc images, memory dumps, and large log sets for anomalies. Instead of reading every file and every line, the investigator begins with a set of prioritized artifacts that deserve attention.

Disc and memory analysis. AI scans disc images to highlight suspicious files, known malware fragments, signs of data staging, and persistence mechanisms such as scheduled tasks, registry modifications, or cron jobs. Memory analysis surfaces injected processes, encryption keys, command-and-control addresses, and lateral-movement artifacts. The speed difference is material: what takes a human forensic analyst days to scan, AI processes in hours.

NLP-driven forensic queries. An investigator faces thousands of log lines and asks, in plain language, for suspicious actions on a server in the last forty-eight hours. The AI responds with abnormal account creation, unusual file transfers to an external IP, and modification of a system file. The investigator follows up for commands executed around that time and gets a clear chain: archiving data into a tar file and copying it via SCP. The data-theft path becomes obvious in seconds, not hours.

Forensic integrity. AI-assisted analysis must not alter evidence, must maintain the chain of custody, and must produce outputs that are reproducible. This means read-only access to forensic images, deterministic processing pipelines where possible, and clear labeling of AI-generated findings versus analyst-confirmed findings. When legal or regulatory proceedings follow an incident, the ability to demonstrate that AI findings were verified by a human and that evidence was handled with integrity is not optional.

The Closed Loop: SSDLC ↔ SOC

The build-run boundary between Chapter 4 (AI-SSDLC) and Chapter 5 (AI-SOC) is where the program either compounds or stalls. A one-directional pipeline—code ships, SOC watches, incidents happen, repeat—does not learn. A closed loop does.

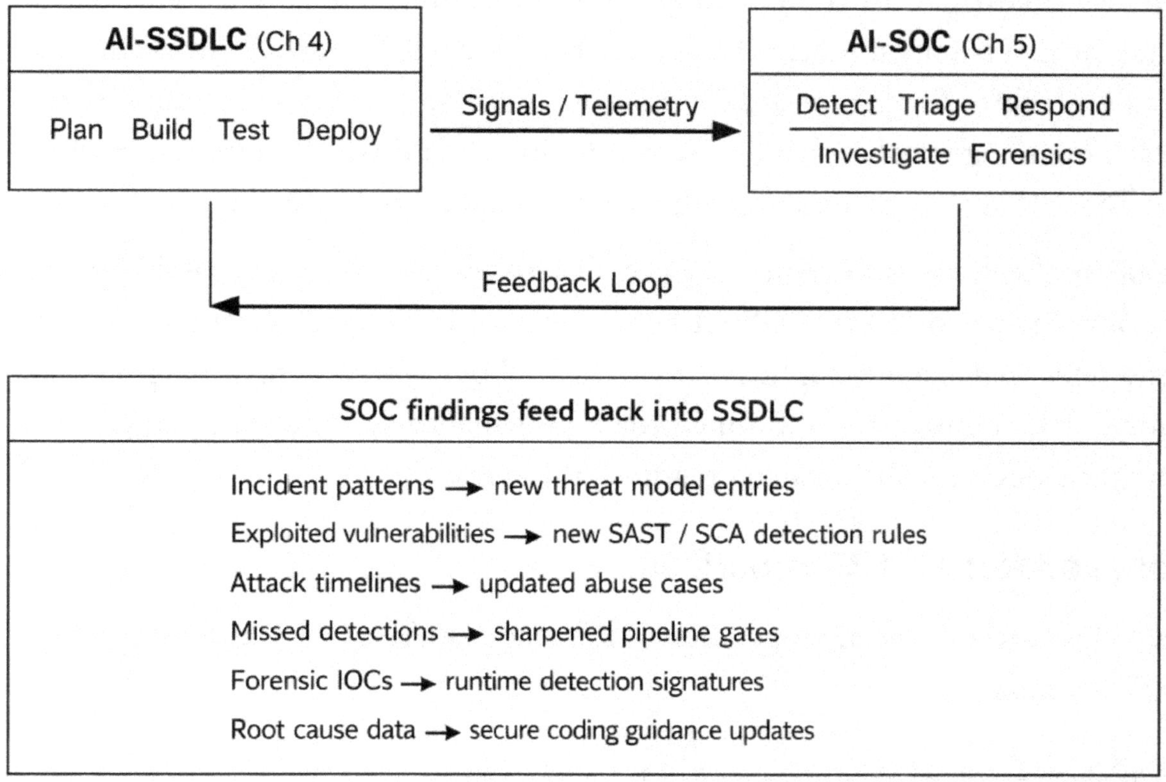

Figure 5.1: The closed loop between AI-SSDLC and AI-SOC. Signals flow both directions; the program compounds when the loop is instrumented.

The loop has specific, measurable outputs. An incident caused by a deserialization vulnerability becomes a new SAST pattern that fires on the next commit touching deserialization code. A forensic finding of a persistence mechanism becomes a runtime detection rule. An attack timeline that showed the SOC missed a signal for four hours becomes a new detection rule with a documented SLA. A root-cause analysis that traced the initial access to a misconfigured IaC template becomes a policy-as-code check in the pipeline.

Programs that instrument this loop—with tickets, tracking, and accountability for each feedback item—improve measurably quarter over quarter. Programs that treat it as aspirational repeat the same incident categories indefinitely.

The Realistic Trajectory: Where AI-SOC Is Heading

Three shifts are likely to define the next two to three years of SOC evolution, and each one carries governance implications alongside capability.

Proactive and predictive operations. SOCs that currently react to incidents will increasingly operate in a mode where AI surfaces pre-attack indicators and recommends pre-emptive actions: tightening a control, revoking a credential, hardening a configuration, or patching a vulnerability before exploitation. This shifts the team's time from firefighting toward risk reduction.

Agent-led investigation is becoming routine. Within the next few years, AI agents conducting the first twenty minutes of every investigation will be normal rather than exceptional. The analyst's role shifts further toward decision, oversight, and exception handling. Organizations that invest now in agent observability, scope discipline, and MCP governance will transition smoothly. Those that skip governance will face incidents caused by the agents themselves.

Human-in-the-loop governance as the differentiator. As AI capability increases, the organizations that perform best will not be the ones with the most autonomous systems. They will be the ones that have thought most carefully about where human judgment adds value, documented those boundaries, and tuned them as evidence accumulates. The HITL spectrum from Chapter 1 does not shrink as AI matures; it refines.

IR Before vs After AI: A Comparison

The table below summarizes the operational difference an AI-SOC makes across key incident-response dimensions.

Table 5.1: Incident response before and after AI-SOC transformation.

Dimension	Traditional SOC	AI-Powered SOC
Detection time	Hours to days	Minutes to hours
Alert triage	Manual, per-alert	Clustered into incidents, auto-prioritized
Investigation	Multi-console, manual pivots	AI-assembled timeline with citations
Containment	Human-initiated, latency in hours	Automated first tier, HITL on high impact
Evidence handling	Inconsistent under pressure	AI-sequenced: capture first, contain second
Root cause	Days to weeks, often incomplete	Hours, cross-surface, with timeline
Reporting	Manual drafts, delayed	AI-drafted, analyst-refined, same day
Learning loop	Post-mortem document, rarely acted on	Instrumented feedback into SSDLC and detection

Case Studies

Case Study 1: AI-Augmented SOC at DEF Logistics

DEF Logistics, a large shipping company with a hybrid environment spanning on-premises data centers and cloud services, faced a common SOC problem: alert volume exceeded capacity.

Their SOC team of five analysts handled around two thousand alerts per day, with many turning out to be false alarms.

They implemented an AI-driven detection platform across their environment, aggregating logs from ships, warehouses, offices, and cloud applications. A notable incident began with a phishing email. A user clicked the link, and the attacker gained a foothold on a workstation. The attacker then moved laterally to a warehouse server and began enumerating it.

The AI system caught unusual behavior at each stage. It flagged the initial login as risky because the employee's login originated from an IP address in another country. It detected the warehouse server running an odd sequence of commands that deviated from baseline operations. It correlated these events into a single incident narrative and alerted the SOC with context that suggested credential compromise and lateral movement. The critical win was correlation—many SOCs see these signals separately; AI connected them and presented a coherent case in minutes.

The attack was contained within thirty minutes with minimal impact. Over six months, the average time to detect dropped from eight hours to under one hour. False positive alerts dropped by roughly fifty-five percent. Analysts reported higher alert quality—one analyst described the change as moving from one useful alert in ten to one useful alert in two. An additional benefit appeared in preventive maintenance: the AI surfaced three misconfigured systems that were not active attacks but still needed fixing, tightening baseline hygiene.

DEF Logistics handled the rollout carefully: an initial parallel-run month, then assist mode where the system suggested actions, then graduated to automatic actions for low-risk, high-confidence scenarios such as disabling clearly compromised accounts. Every automated action opened a ticket with documentation for governance and traceability.

Case Study 2: Automated Incident Response at XYZ Bank

XYZ Bank implemented an automation platform with AI capabilities to manage high alert volume and improve incident response. One afternoon, monitoring flagged unusual database queries on a credit card database, and endpoint protection flagged a suspicious process on an application server. These two signals could have been treated as separate issues. The AI correlation engine linked them and classified the situation as a potential data breach, identifying the application server as the pivot point into the database.

The automated response sequence began immediately. The system isolated the application server from the network, suspended the database user account being abused, alerted the on-call IR team with a clear summary of involved systems and actions already taken, and captured a memory snapshot and relevant logs to preserve volatile evidence. By the time the team assembled within thirty minutes, the AI had produced a timeline: intrusion via a deserialization vulnerability on the server, privilege escalation, then database access using stolen credentials, with an estimate of records likely accessed based on query logs.

The team verified containment, patched the vulnerable component, rotated potentially compromised credentials, and briefed management. The system produced a draft incident report that the lead analyst refined and sent to the CISO the same evening. XYZ Bank contained the breach in under an hour. Mean time to respond dropped from roughly eight hours to one and a half hours in the quarter after deployment.

The leadership lesson: speed is part tooling and part operating model. The tooling executes fast, and the model succeeds because the team defined the response sequence, maintained readiness, and trusted automation for specific, bounded actions.

Case Study 3: Cross-Surface Forensics After a Supply-Chain Incident

A healthcare technology provider serving hospital networks discovered, through anomalous outbound traffic detected by the AI-SOC, that a background service on several customer-facing servers was communicating with an unfamiliar external endpoint. The traffic volume was low—a few kilobytes every six hours—and had been running for eleven days before the behavioral model flagged it as statistically deviant for that workload class.

The forensics investigation was where AI earned its place. The team needed to answer three questions fast: what communication was carried out, how it got there, and which customer environments were affected.

The AI forensics platform correlated across four surfaces simultaneously. It traced the background service to a legitimate dependency that had been updated through the standard build pipeline. It then inspected the dependency's provenance and found that the update had introduced a small network module does not present in the prior version. Code-level analysis by the AI identified the module as a data collector that extracted server metadata and limited patient-scheduling identifiers, encrypted them, and transmitted them to the external endpoint on a timer.

Identity telemetry showed that the build pipeline's service account had pulled the dependency update from the public registry, and the registry's package history showed that the maintainer account had changed ownership four weeks earlier—the same pattern flagged in Chapter 4's CI/CD case study, but in this case, it was not caught pre-deployment.

The AI assembled a complete timeline: ownership transfer of the package, new release with the embedded module, automated pull through the pipeline, deployment to twelve customer-facing servers across three hospital networks, and eleven days of low-volume data collection. The human forensic team validated the timeline, confirmed no clinical data was exfiltrated (the module collected scheduling metadata, not health records), and worked with legal and the affected hospitals on notification and remediation.

The closed-loop outcome was immediate. The dependency was removed and replaced. The build pipeline added package-maintainer-change detection as a blocking gate. A new SAST rule was created to flag imported modules that introduce network calls do not present in the prior version. The SOC added a detection for the specific exfiltration pattern. And the provider's vendor-management process was updated to monitor open-source maintainer continuity for critical dependencies.

The lesson is that AI-powered forensics across code, infrastructure, identity, and application telemetry turns a slow, painful investigation into a fast, thorough one—and the closed loop ensures that the same class of incident does not repeat. Without the cross-surface correlation, the eleven-day dwell time could easily have stretched to months.

KPIs to Track

AI-SOC programs strengthen when leaders measure detection, response, and learning together.

Mean time to detect (MTTD). Track from event occurrence to alert surfacing, segmented by incident category. A move from eight hours to under one hour on identity-driven incidents is a strong signal. Use red-team simulations to validate that detection times hold against adversarial behavior.

Mean time to contain (MTTC). Track from alert to containment action. Sub-metrics include time to isolate affected systems and time to disable compromised accounts. Expect sharp reductions after automation matures for first-tier actions.

False positive rate by source. Track precision for each telemetry source: email, endpoint, identity, cloud, application. A downward trend indicates tuning success. When the rate plateaus high, allocate effort to data quality or model recalibration for that source specifically.

Detection rate against red-team exercises. Track the percentage of simulated attack scenarios the AI-SOC catches. A rising trend indicates learning. When a red team can simulate exfiltration without triggering detection, treat it as a priority gap.

Dwell time. Track how long an attacker remains in the environment before detection and containment. Aim to shrink this continuously; some organizations have moved from weeks to hours with AI-augmented detection.

Automated action execution and accuracy. Track how often the system autonomously prevents an issue and track success versus erroneous actions. This KPI ties directly to prevention value and automation maturity.

Investigation time. Track time from detection to root-cause establishment and impact scoping. AI should compress this through correlation and evidence processing. Post-incident report readiness within the same business day is a practical milestone.

Closed-loop feedback items actioned. Track the number of SOC findings that produce a concrete SSDLC improvement (new SAST rule, new pipeline gate, updated threat model, new detection signature) within thirty days of incident closure. A low number signals that the loop is aspirational, not instrumented.

Risks and Guardrails

AI-SOC introduces predictable risks alongside speed and scale. Guardrails keep the system effective and safe.

Initial tuning period. AI models need calibration. If deployed without tuning, they overwhelm analysts or miss obvious issues. The guardrail is a planned calibration phase using historical data, adjustment of anomaly thresholds, and close review of early findings.

Over-automation and blast-radius control. Autonomous response can prevent spread and can cause harm when it triggers the wrong action on a critical system. Isolating a domain controller due to a false alert creates an outage. The guardrail is stepwise automation maturity: notifications first, then human approval, then automation for low-risk, high-confidence actions, with an override mechanism.

Adversary evasion. Attackers can study detection patterns and behave in ways that avoid triggering AI. Guardrails include continuous model updates, a mix of detection methods (AI, rules, threat intelligence, deception), and honeypots that lure attackers into revealing themselves.

Excessive agency in SOC agents. An SOC agent with access to SIEM, EDR, identity provider, and firewall can cause significant damage if manipulated or if its scope is too broad. The guardrail is a least-privilege tool access per agent, scoped MCP connections, logged tool calls, and human-in-the-loop gates on any action that modifies production controls.

Data quality and feed completeness. AI detection develops blind spots when logs are missing or normalization is inconsistent. The guardrail is monitoring the data pipeline itself: alert when a feed goes silent, validate that timestamps and identities align, and track coverage gaps.

Evidence destruction through premature containment. Rebooting a machine before capturing memory destroys volatile artifacts. The guardrail is sequenced response: evidence capture first, containment second, enforced by the automation platform.

Analysts trust calibration. AI outputs fail if analysts distrust them and create risk if analysts overtrust them. The guardrail is training on how the AI works, transparency on why alerts were raised, performance-metric sharing, AI-off drills, and a culture of validate-and-escalate.

Forensic integrity. AI-assisted analysis that alters evidence or produces non-reproducible findings is a liability. The guardrail is read-only access to forensic images, deterministic processing, clear labeling of AI-generated versus analyst-confirmed findings, and chain-of-custody controls.

Executive Takeaways

- **The AI-SOC exists because the math demands it.** Event volume exceeds human capacity, attack signals are quieter than the noise, and manual workflows create latency the attacker exploits. AI absorbs volume, correlates signals, and executes bounded response at machine speed.
- **Detection value comes from cross-surface correlation.** The six surfaces from Chapter 1 each generate telemetry. AI's unique advantage is connecting weak signals across them into coherent incident narratives in seconds.
- **Agentic AI is arriving in the SOC.** Agents that investigate, enrich, and recommend will become routine. Govern them now: least-privilege MCP connections, non-human identity hygiene, logged tool calls, and HITL gates on destructive actions.
- **HITL tiering keeps response safe.** Fully automated for narrow, reversible, high-confidence actions. Human-on-the-loop for bounded actions. Human-in-the-loop required for broad or irreversible actions. Document the tiering and tune as trust accumulates.
- **Forensics is a first-class capability, not an afterthought.** AI-assisted forensics across code, identity, infrastructure, and application telemetry turns slow investigations into fast, thorough ones. Forensic integrity is non-negotiable.
- **The closed loop separates mature programs from reactive ones.** SOC findings feed back into SSDLC as new threat models, detection rules, pipeline gates, and secure coding guidance. Instrument the loop and track items actioned.
- **Measure detection, response, and learning together.** MTTD, MTTC, false positive rate, dwell time, red-team detection rate, automated action accuracy, investigation time, and closed-loop feedback items actioned—reviewed on a cadence.

- **Preparedness determines whether AI-SOC delivers.** Data sources, response sequences, evidence-handling rules, agent governance, and team training need to be set up before a crisis.

End-of-Chapter Reflection Questions

- For the last five significant incidents your SOC handled, how many hours elapsed between the first signal and confirmed containment? Where did the most time go—detection, triage, approval, or execution?
- If you turned off AI-assisted detection tomorrow and relied only on rules and signatures, which attack categories would go undetected, and for how long?
- Which of your SOC tools currently operate as agents—that is, they take actions autonomously—and do they have least-privilege tool access, scoped credentials, and logged tool calls?
- When was the last time a red-team exercise specifically tested whether your AI-SOC could detect and respond to a simulated attack? What was the result?
- For the last incident where forensics was required, was the evidence captured before or after containment actions? Is that sequencing enforced automatically, or does it depend on analyst memory?
- How many SOC findings from the last quarter produced a concrete SSDLC improvement—a new detection rule, a new SAST pattern, an updated threat model, or a pipeline gate? What would it take to double that number?
- If an AI agent in your SOC were manipulated through prompt injections to revoke access for a legitimate administrator, what would stop it? At what layer would the defense activate?
- Which three KPIs from this chapter, if you started reviewing them monthly with your SOC leadership, would most sharpen the program over the next year?

Chapter 6

IDENTITY, DATA, SAAS, AND AI SECURITY–THE ADAPTIVE CONTROL PLANE

Four Surfaces, One Operating Model

Chapter 1 introduced six security surfaces. Four of them—identity, data, SaaS, and AI itself—share a structural property that separates them from code and endpoint security: they are surfaces where static, rule-based controls have stopped being sufficient and where AI-driven, context-aware, continuously evaluating controls have become the operating pattern. A firewall rule either allows or blocks. An identity decision in a modern environment needs to consider who, from where, on what device, at what time, accessing what data, with what privilege, in what behavioral context—and re-evaluate continuously as any of those factors change.

This chapter treats all four as a unified control plane. Identity governs who. Data governs what. SaaS governs where. AI security governs the intelligent systems themselves. In each domain, the lens is the same: what are the risks that matter, and how does AI help address them in ways static controls cannot? The chapter is deliberately practical. If a control does not produce a measurable outcome or address a real failure mode, it does not appear here.

Identity Security: How AI Helps

Identity sits at the center of almost every serious incident. Credentials, tokens, session handling, privilege sprawl, and non-human identities such as service accounts, CI/CD tokens, and AI agent credentials are the connective tissue of modern breaches. The question is no longer whether to invest in identity security; it is how to make identity controls adaptive, continuous, and scalable.

Adaptive authentication. AI evaluates each login using risk signals—device reputation, location patterns, login timing, IP reputation, breach exposure data—and adjusts friction accordingly. Low-risk logins proceed smoothly. High-risk logins trigger step-up verification or block. The result is fewer successful credential-theft incidents and less user friction during routine access. Organizations deploying risk-based authentication report blocking or challenging upwards of ninety-five percent of compromised login attempts automatically.

Continuous session evaluation. Authentication at login is necessary but not sufficient. Session hijacking, token theft, and insider misuse occur after a valid login. AI monitors in-session behavior—unusual data access patterns, privilege escalation, lateral movement to unfamiliar systems—and can require re-authentication or terminate a session when behavior deviates from the user's established baseline. This is zero trust applied to sessions, not just to login.

Privilege governance and access analytics. Permissions accumulate faster than they are revoked. AI compares access granted against access actually used, flags dormant accounts, excessive privileges, and toxic permission combinations such as the ability to both initiate and approve transactions. One large enterprise discovered that thirty percent of privileges could be removed with zero business impact by clustering users by function and identifying outliers. The reduction shrinks the attack surface and simplifies compliance evidence.

Non-human identity management. Service accounts, API keys, CI/CD tokens, and AI agent credentials are identities with the same rights and risks as human users—often with broader permissions and less oversight. AI helps by profiling expected behavior for each non-human identity, flagging deviations, enforcing rotation policies, and correlating non-human identity activity with broader incident signals. Chapter 5's healthcare forensics case study began with a dormant contractor service account; the root cause was a non-human identity lifecycle gap.

Customer identity and fraud prevention. Customer-facing identity systems face credential stuffing, account takeover, fake account creation, and bot-driven abuse at scale. AI detects these patterns across device fingerprints, IP ranges, and behavioral signals, scoring each login and transaction for risk. One financial services firm saw a forty-percent reduction in account takeover fraud after deploying AI-driven risk scoring on customer logins.

Data Security: How AI Helps

Data is the ultimate target of most breaches—customer records, financial data, intellectual property, regulated health information, and model training sets. The challenge is that data is no longer neatly contained in databases behind firewalls. It lives in cloud storage, SaaS applications, collaboration tools, AI prompts, model outputs, local notebooks, and export files. Traditional DLP addressed a narrower surface; the modern data estate requires AI to see what rules cannot.

Automated data classification. Most organizations cannot classify their data at scale using manual tagging. AI-driven classifiers scan unstructured stores—documents, emails, chat messages, code repositories, cloud storage buckets—and identify regulated data (PII, PHI, PCI, trade secrets) based on content analysis, not file metadata. The classification then feeds downstream controls: access policies, encryption requirements, retention rules, and monitoring sensitivity.

Context-aware data loss prevention. Classical DLP relies on patterns—credit card numbers, social security formats—and produces high false-positive rates because the same patterns appear in legitimate documents. AI-enhanced DLP adds context: who is sending the data, to where, for what apparent purpose, and whether this matches the user's role and recent activity. The result is fewer blocked legitimate transfers and more caught real exfiltration attempts.

Shadow AI data flow detection. Chapter 1 introduced the Shadow AI pattern—employees pasting sensitive data into unsanctioned AI services. AI helps detect this by monitoring egress traffic for AI service endpoints, correlating volume and frequency with data sensitivity classifications, and flagging patterns that suggest regulated data is leaving through prompt-based channels. Proxy-level visibility, combined with classification, turns Shadow AI from an unmeasured risk into a measurable and manageable one.

Data lineage and movement tracking. Where did this data come from, where has it been, and where is it going? AI-assisted lineage tools map data flows across systems, including flows through AI pipelines—from training data ingestion through model output to downstream consumption. This visibility supports privacy compliance (DPDPA, GDPR), audit readiness, and incident scoping when a breach occurs.

Access anomaly detection on sensitive datastores. AI monitors who access sensitive data, when, from where, and how much. A query against a patient records database at 2 AM from an account that normally touches only billing data generates a high-risk signal. Combined with the identity signals from the previous section, data-access anomaly detection catches exfiltration attempts that bypass network-layer controls entirely.

SaaS Security: How AI Helps

SaaS adoption has grown faster than security visibility into it. The average enterprise uses hundreds of SaaS applications, and IT or security teams have sanctioned a fraction of them. Each application holds a subset of corporate data, has its own identity layer, its own API permissions, and its own sharing and export capabilities. The result is a surface that is large, distributed, and under-governed.

SaaS posture management. AI-driven SaaS Security Posture Management (SSPM) tools continuously evaluate configurations across the SaaS estate—sharing settings, authentication requirements, API permissions, data-export capabilities, admin-role assignments—and surface drift from secure baselines. AI prioritizes findings by business impact and exploitability, so the team fixes what matters rather than working through an alphabetical list.

SaaS sprawl and shadow SaaS discovery. Employees adopt SaaS tools organically, often authenticating through OAuth or SSO and granting broad permission without security review. AI identifies shadow SaaS by analyzing OAuth token grants, SSO authentication logs, and network traffic patterns. The output is a continuously updated inventory of all SaaS applications in use, with risk scoring based on data access, user count, and permission scope.

SaaS-to-SaaS connection risk. Modern SaaS environments create hidden trust chains through integrations—a project management tool connected to a file storage tool connected to a communication tool, each with OAuth tokens granting data access. AI maps these connections, identifies over-privileged integrations, and flags when a new connection grants access that exceeds what the business workflow requires. A compromised SaaS-to-SaaS integration is a lateral movement path that never touches the corporate network.

User activity monitoring across SaaS. AI extends UEBA into the SaaS layer. Unusual download volumes from a cloud file store, mass sharing of folders with external accounts, admin-role assignments by non-admin users, and bulk exports from CRM or HR systems—these patterns are visible when the SaaS estate is instrumented and monitored. The signals feed into the AI-SOC (Chapter 5) for correlation with identity and endpoint events.

AI Security: How AI Helps Secure AI

AI systems are now assets that need securing, not just tools that provide security. An organization that deploys models, agents, RAG pipelines, and MCP-connected tools has a new surface that did not exist five years ago, and most security programs are still building controls for it from scratch.

AI inventory and lifecycle governance. The first control is knowing what you have. AI helps by discovering models, agents, and AI-powered features across the estate through API analysis, cloud resource scanning, and SaaS integration mapping. The output is an AI asset register—which models are deployed, where they run, what data they access, who owns them, and what human-oversight boundaries apply. Without this, governance is aspirational.

Prompt and output safety. Input and output classifiers detect prompt injection attempts, sensitive data in prompts, unsafe outputs, and policy violations before they reach users or downstream systems. These classifiers are themselves AI systems, creating a layered defense where one model monitors another. The OWASP Top 10 for LLM (Chapter 2) maps directly to the control set: prompt injection defense (LLM01), sensitive information filtering (LLM02), output handling (LLM05), and system prompt protection (LLM07).

Agent access governance. AI agents—coding assistants, SOC investigation agents, customer-support agents, workflow automation agents—hold credentials and make tool calls.

AI helps govern agents by profiling expected tool-call patterns, flagging anomalous agent behavior, enforcing least-privilege tool access, and alerting when an agent's scope creeps beyond its intended boundaries. MCP servers, as Chapter 2 described, are the connective tissue; governing MCP access is how agent scope is controlled in practice.

Model and data supply-chain integrity. Foundation models, fine-tuning datasets, RAG corpora, and adapters are supply-chain assets. AI assists with provenance verification, integrity checking, and continuous monitoring for drift or poisoning. The same supply-chain discipline Chapter 4 applied to code dependencies—SBOM, signed artifacts, continuous verification—applies to model and data assets.

AI red-teaming feedback integration. Chapter 2 introduced AI red-teaming. The findings from red-team exercises flow into the AI security control plane as updated input filters, tightened output classifiers, adjusted agent permissions, and new detection signatures in the SOC. AI helps automate the regression-testing of known attack vectors so previously patched weaknesses do not reappear after model updates.

How AI Helps: A Cross-Domain View

The table below summarizes how AI contributes across all four domains, reinforcing the unified control-plane framing.

Table 6.1: How AI helps across identity, data, SaaS, and AI security. The adaptive control plane applies the same operating model to all four surfaces.

Domain	Key Risks	How AI Helps
Identity	Credential theft, session hijack, privilege sprawl, non-human identity gaps	Adaptive auth, continuous session evaluation, privilege analytics, NHI profiling, fraud detection
Data	Exfiltration, shadow AI data flows, unclassified stores, privacy violations	Automated classification, context-aware DLP, shadow AI detection, lineage tracking, access anomaly detection
SaaS	Misconfiguration, sprawl, shadow SaaS, SaaS-to-SaaS trust chains, bulk export	SSPM, OAuth/SSO discovery, integration mapping, cross-SaaS UEBA, risk-scored inventory
AI Systems	Prompt injection, model theft, agent overreach, supply-chain poisoning, unregistered models	AI inventory, prompt/output classifiers, agent behavior profiling, model provenance, red-team regression

Case Study: Adaptive Authentication and SaaS Governance at SecureBank

SecureBank implemented AI-driven adaptive authentication for both online banking customers and employees. Every login attempt received a risk score from 0 to 100 based on device, location, user behavior baseline, IP reputation, and breach exposure. Low-risk login required only the password. Medium-risk logins required MFA. High-risk logins were blocked or required a stronger verification path.

Employee results were immediate. The number of daily MFA challenges dropped by sixty percent because routine logins were classified as low risk. At the same time, the system blocked fifteen malicious login attempts in the first quarter—cases where the password was correct, but context signals were wrong, such as overseas logins for users who rarely traveled. For online banking customers, fraud incidents due to account takeover dropped by seventy percent year over year.

SecureBank also applied AI to privilege governance. The system flagged contractor accounts retaining access months after projects ended, and operations team members holding admin rights they never used. Roughly three hundred accounts were downgraded or revoked, shrinking the insider threat surface while keeping operations moving.

In the same program, the security team extended AI-driven visibility into the SaaS estate. An OAuth-based discovery identified forty-three SaaS applications that employees had connected via SSO without security review. Seven of those held regulated customer data, and three had SaaS-to-SaaS integrations granting broad read access to the corporate file store. The team revoked over-privileged integrations, added the high-risk applications to a sanctioned-or-blocked list, and implemented ongoing SSPM monitoring so new connections would surface automatically rather than during annual audits.

The combined lesson is that identity, data, and SaaS security reinforce each other. Adaptive authentication reduces credential compromise. Privilege governance reduces blast radius. SaaS discovery closes the visibility gap. And AI is the common enabler across all three—making continuous, context-aware evaluation practical at enterprise scale.

KPIs to Track

KPIs across the four domains share a common structure: measure risk reduction, measure coverage, and measure the effectiveness of AI-driven controls.

Identity. Account compromises prevented; MFA challenge rate and false-challenge rate; privileges removed as a percentage of total; non-human identity coverage (percentage with defined lifecycle and monitoring); insider-threat incidents linked to credential misuse.

Data. Percentage of critical data stores classified; shadow AI data-loss events detected; mean time from classification to policy enforcement; lineage coverage for regulated data; false-positive rate on DLP actions.

SaaS. Number of sanctioned versus unsanctioned SaaS applications; SaaS-to-SaaS integrations reviewed versus total; percentage of SaaS applications meeting hardened configuration baselines; time to detect and remediate new shadow SaaS connections.

AI Systems. Percentage of deployed AI systems in the AI inventory with documented owners; prompt-injection detection rate on production systems; percentage of AI agents with defined HITL boundaries; time from red-team finding to control update; model evaluation freshness.

A strong practice reviews these together, because the domains interact. A compromised identity accesses sensitive data through an unsanctioned SaaS application connected to an ungoverned AI agent—that is one incident spanning all four surfaces, and the KPIs should make the gap visible before the incident does.

Risks and Guardrails

User friction versus security. Adaptive controls that are too sensitive create fatigue and workarounds. The guardrail is an ongoing review of challenge rates and outcomes, paired with continuous tuning based on true positives, false positives, and user feedback.

Privacy and monitoring scope. Behavioral monitoring across identity and data can raise employee and customer privacy concerns. Guardrails include transparency about what is monitored and why, narrow scope aligned to security purpose, strict use limitations, and alignment with DPDPA, GDPR, and local privacy requirements.

Bias in risk scoring. Models can inadvertently challenge certain populations more—users from specific regions, roles that travel frequently, and teams with unusual working patterns. The guardrail is a continuous evaluation of denial and challenge rates by subgroup, personalization through user baselines, and a clear escalation path for legitimate users.

SaaS integration blind spots. New SaaS-to-SaaS connections can appear daily. The guardrail is continuous OAuth and SSO monitoring, so new connections surface in real time, not at the next quarterly review.

AI engine as a target. The adaptive risk engine itself becomes a high-value target. Guardrails include strong admin authentication, restricted access, audit logging of policy changes, change management for model updates, and monitoring for anomalies in the engine's own decisions.

Fail-safe design. When the risk engine is unavailable, the organization needs a defined fallback. Many choose a fail-secure posture that increases verification during outages, with redundancy and fallback policies tested before they are needed.

Executive Takeaways

- **Identity, data, SaaS, and AI security share one operating model.** Context-aware, continuously evaluating, AI-driven controls work across all four surfaces. Build the control plane once; apply it consistently.
- **Identity remains the connective tissue of most breaches.** Adaptive authentication, continuous session evaluation, privilege governance, and non-human identity management are where AI delivers the most immediate ROI.
- **Data security has expanded beyond the database.** AI classification, context-aware DLP, shadow AI detection, and lineage tracking address a data surface that now includes prompts, model outputs, and SaaS exports.
- **SaaS is the fastest-growing blind spot.** AI-driven discovery, posture management, and SaaS-to-SaaS integration monitoring close the visibility gap that manual inventories cannot.
- **AI systems are assets that need securing.** Inventory, prompt/output safety, agent governance, model supply-chain integrity, and red-team feedback integration are the control set. Start with inventory and access controls; expand as the surface matures.
- **The domains reinforce each other.** A compromised identity that accesses sensitive data through an unsanctioned SaaS application connected to an ungoverned AI agent is one incident spanning all four surfaces. Measure and govern accordingly.
- **Measure risk reduction, coverage, and AI-control effectiveness together.** KPIs across identity, data, SaaS, and AI systems should be reviewed on a single cadence because the domains interact.
- **Governance is the differentiator.** The technology is available. Privacy discipline, bias monitoring, fail-safe design, and clear human-oversight boundaries are what make it trustworthy.

End-of-Chapter Reflection Questions

- For every non-human identity in your environment—service accounts, API keys, CI/CD tokens, AI agent credentials—is there a defined owner, a rotation policy, and monitoring for behavioral deviation?

- What percentage of your critical data stores have AI-assisted classification in place? For the unclassified stores, what is the plan and timeline?
- How many SaaS applications are in use across the organization, how many are sanctioned, and how many SaaS-to-SaaS integrations have been reviewed in the last ninety days?
- If you ran a prompt-injection test against your production AI systems today, which system would detect it and which would not? Which would log it for SOC review?
- Does your adaptive authentication system produce different false-challenge rates for different user populations? Have you measured this, and what would you do with the data?
- For the AI agents operating in your environment, can you list the credentials each holds, the tools each can access, and the HITL boundaries each operate under?
- How does a data-access anomaly signal from your data security controls reach the SOC, and how does the SOC's investigation feed back into access policy?
- If a regulator asked how, you govern the AI systems influencing identity, data, and SaaS decisions—including who owns each, how each is evaluated, and where human oversight applies—could you produce that evidence within a day?

Part 3

ADVANCED TOPICS & GOVERNANCE

Chapter 7

ADVERSARIAL AI AND EMERGING RISKS

When Defenders Use AI, Attackers Learn Faster Too

Earlier chapters focused on what AI unlocks for defense—faster detection, smarter triage, continuous code review, adaptive authentication, and cross-surface correlation. This chapter faces the other side of that coin. Attackers use AI as a productivity engine to scale classic tactics. Attackers target AI systems directly to degrade, manipulate, or subvert them. And as AI-driven defenses mature, adversaries adapt techniques specifically designed to exploit the way models learn, reason, and act.

The practical takeaway for a leader reads simply. Treat AI systems as security-critical assets, with the same discipline used for identity, software, and networks. When that discipline is present, AI becomes a durable advantage. When the discipline is missing, AI becomes a new surface an adversary can test and eventually exploit. This chapter provides the threat taxonomy, the real-world examples, and the defensive patterns that keep the advantage on the right side.

The Three Layers of Adversarial AI Risk

Adversarial AI risk operates on three distinct layers, each demanding different controls.

Layer 1—Attackers weaponize AI. Generative models draft phishing at scale with clean language and cultural fluency. Voice synthesis impersonates executives during payment approvals. Code-generation models accelerate exploit development and vulnerability discovery. Reconnaissance tools scrape, summarize, and target based on public data. Earlier chapters covered the defensive response—AI-driven detection, identity verification, HITL on high-impact decisions. This chapter focuses on understanding the attacker's accelerating capability, so defenders stay calibrated.

Layer 2—Attackers evade AI defenses. Once an AI-driven defense is in place, adversaries probe it. They learn what the model "sees" through experimentation, adjust inputs until they pass detection boundaries, and iterate faster when they have access to similar models publicly. This is evasion—the adversarial-examples problem applied to production security tooling.

Layer 3—Attackers target AI systems directly. The AI stack itself becomes the target. Training data poisoning alters what the model learns. Model theft through API querying gives attackers an offline copy to practice against. Prompt injections manipulate agent behavior. Data extraction coaxes sensitive training data into outputs. Denial-of-wallet attacks drive inference costs into the stratosphere. These are not theoretical—they are operational attack patterns with real tooling and real incidents.

The three layers are not mutually exclusive. A sophisticated adversary can weaponize AI to scale phishing (Layer 1), craft evasion payloads against the target's AI email filter (Layer 2), and poison the feedback loop by flooding the filter with adversarial samples that degrade its performance over time (Layer 3). Defensive planning that treats any single layer as "the adversarial AI problem" misses two-thirds of the risk.

Insights and Practical Frameworks

Evasion: How Attackers Slip Past AI Defenses

A model learns statistical patterns and makes decisions based on them. Evasion exploits the boundaries of those patterns. In cybersecurity, evasion takes three common forms.

Feature-space manipulation. A malware author pads a malicious binary with benign-looking byte sequences copied from legitimate software. The model's feature extraction picks up the added "goodware" signals and mislabels the file. The payload is unchanged; the wrapping fools the classifier. This is the adversarial-example problem applied to real malware, and it has been demonstrated repeatedly against commercial classifiers.

Content-level evasion. A phishing operator strips obvious cues from messages. Instead of a link-laden email, the attacker sends a short, context-free message—"Hi, are you available? I need a quick task"—that carries no link, no attachment, and no suspicious keywords. The AI email filter has a few features to score. The employee replies, and the attacker moves the conversation into a channel with weaker controls. The defense is not to make the filter smarter alone; it is to train employees that unexpected, context-free requests from external domains are a verification trigger, and to treat vague-availability emails as a distinct risk category in the model's policy.

Slow-and-low exfiltration. If an AI-driven DLP system flags rapid data transfers, an attacker exfiltrates slowly—a few hundred records at a time, during business hours, mimicking normal application traffic. Chapter 5's healthcare forensics case study described exactly this pattern: small-batch exfiltration by a dormant service account that looked like legitimate application behavior to any single-event rule. The defense is a behavioral baseline combined with cumulative-volume alerts, not just single-event thresholds.

The meta-lesson across all three forms is defense-in-depth. A single AI detection layer, no matter how accurate, has exploitable boundaries. Layer detection AI plus rules, plus behavioral analytics, plus deception (honeypots and canary tokens), plus human verification on high-impact actions—means the attacker has to beat multiple independent systems, not one.

Poisoning: Corrupting What the Model Learns

Poisoning attacks target the training pipeline. If an attacker can influence what the model learns, they can bias it toward missing specific patterns or embed a hidden trigger that causes misclassification on command.

Label poisoning. An attacker compromises a system that generates training labels—for example, the ticketing system that marks incidents as resolved or false-positive. By flipping labels on a targeted subset of malicious events from "attack" to "benign," the attacker teaches the model that a specific attack pattern is normal. The next time the pattern appears in production, the model stays silent. The defense is restricting who can influence labels, validating datasets for statistical anomalies, and cross-verifying labels against independent signals before retraining.

Backdoor insertion. An attacker contributes a poisoned model, adapter, or dataset to a public repository. The model performs normally on standard inputs but misclassifies any input containing a specific trigger token or sequence. A security product that integrates the poisoned component inherits the backdoor. The defense is the model supply-chain discipline from Chapter 4—provenance verification, integrity checks, testing against known poisoning signatures, and treating model updates like software releases.

Feedback-loop pollution. Many security tools retrain on their own outputs. If an attacker can flood the system with adversarial samples that get classified as benign and fed back into training, the model drifts toward missing similar samples in the future. The defense is controlled retraining with human review of samples that influence the training set, and monitoring for distribution shifts that do not match expected changes in the environment.

Model Theft, Extraction, and Privacy Attacks

Models can leak value in two directions: intellectual property outward and training data outward.

Model extraction. When a model is exposed through an API, an attacker can query it systematically and build an approximate copy. The copy lets the attacker test evasion payloads offline until they pass, without alerting the defender's monitoring. The defense is rate-limiting, query-pattern monitoring, output perturbation (adding controlled noise to outputs), and treating model APIs as sensitive endpoints with the same access controls applied to any privileged service.

Membership inference. An attacker queries the model with a specific data point and observes the confidence of the response. If the model is more confident in the data it was trained on, the attacker can infer whether a specific record was in the training set. For a medical model, this can reveal whether a specific patient's data was used. For a security model, this can reveal which incidents the organization has experienced. The defense is differential privacy during training, confidence calibration, and limiting the precision of output scores.

Training-data extraction. Clever prompting can coax fragments of training data from a model—names, addresses, code snippets, internal system details—especially when guardrails are weak. This is LLM02 (Sensitive Information Disclosure) from the OWASP Top 10 for LLM (Chapter 2). The defense is minimizing sensitive data in training, output filtering, and red-team probing that specifically tests for data leakage before deployment and on a cadence post-deployment.

Prompt Injection and Agent Manipulation

Prompt injection is the defining attack class of the LLM era. It deserves focused treatment here because it directly threatens the agent-based architecture covered in Chapters 2, 4, 5, and 6.

Direct prompt injection. An attacker provides input designed to override the system prompt and redirect the model's behavior. Against a standalone chat model, this might produce unsafe content. Against an agent with tool access, it can trigger real-world actions—exfiltrating data through an MCP-connected tool, making API calls with the agent's credentials, and modifying files the agent has access to. The severity scales with the agent's scope: the more tools and credentials the agent holds, the higher the blast radius of a successful injection.

Indirect prompt injection. An attacker embeds instructions in content the agent will read—a support ticket, an email body, a document retrieved through RAG, a webpage fetched through MCP. The agent processes the content, encounters the injected instruction, and executes it as if it were part of its task. This is particularly dangerous because the attacker never interacts with the model directly; the attack travels through trusted data channels. The defense is treating all retrieved content as untrusted, applying input sanitization on the MCP data path, and placing HITL on tool calls that modify state.

Tool-use abuse. Even without prompt injection, an agent can be manipulated into using its tools in unintended ways through carefully crafted inputs that exploit the model's reasoning.

This is OWASP LLM06 (Excessive Agency) in practice. The defense is least-privilege tool scoping—every agent receives the minimum tools, permissions, and credentials required for its defined task—combined with output validation on tool calls and human approval on destructive actions.

Deepfakes and Synthetic Identity: Attacking Human Trust

Deepfakes target human trust rather than technical boundaries. When a voice sounds like an executive and the message matches the current business context, a staff member can act fast and skip verification. In a widely reported incident, criminals used an AI-generated voice to impersonate a senior executive and instruct an employee to execute a high-value wire transfer. The employee complied because the voice, the context, and the urgency were all convincing.

The defense cannot rely on "spotting the fake" alone. Detection tools help, but deepfakes improve faster than detection, and humans vary in their ability to identify manipulation under pressure. Safer strategy upgrades the process. Callback verification on known numbers, not the number the caller provides. Multi-person approval for high-value transfers. Contextual challenges that a pre-recorded deepfake cannot answer. And one structural change that removes the largest chunk of deepfake risk: voice stops being an authentication channel. Voice can remain a communication channel; voice-only approval paths for sensitive actions are retired.

Autonomous Offensive Agents: The Forward Trajectory

Agentic AI is not exclusively a defensive capability. Offensive agents—systems that can autonomously enumerate targets, test credentials, exploit vulnerabilities, move laterally, and adapt based on what they find—are an active area of research and a near-term operational reality. Security competitions have already featured machine-speed cyber exercises. Commercially available offensive security tools incorporate agent-driven testing. The timeline between "weakness exists" and "proof of concept exists" is compressing.

The defensive implications are practical. Patch discipline, asset inventory, and exposure management become more urgent because surprise windows shrink. Runtime sensors (Chapter 4) and cross-surface correlation (Chapter 5) become essential because autonomous agents produce less noise than human operators and move faster. AI red-teaming (Chapter 2) becomes non-optional because the adversary's test cadence is continuous. And the closed-loop feedback between SSDLC and SOC (Chapters 4–5) becomes the mechanism that keeps defenders adapting at a pace that matches the adversary.

Defend the AI Lifecycle: A Working Model

To keep adversarial risk actionable, apply a lifecycle lens with three phases.

Build. Secure and curate training data. Restrict who can influence model updates. Validate datasets for anomalies and known poisoning signatures. Document training sets and maintain the chain of custody for model artifacts. Treat model artifacts as sensitive assets.

Deploy. Limit model exposure. Enforce access controls on APIs and MCP connections. Rate-limit and monitor for extraction-style querying. Log all prompts and outputs as security telemetry. Apply input and output classifiers for prompt injection and data leakage. Treat deployment like a production software release—with review, testing, and rollback readiness.

Operate. Monitor drift. Run adversarial tests on a cadence. Perform AI red-teaming (Chapter 2). Retrain through controlled releases with human review of training-data changes. Keep humans in the loop for high-impact decisions influenced by model outputs. Treat AI incidents—poisoning, evasion bypass, agent compromise—like any other high-impact security event, with root-cause analysis and feedback into the build phase.

Adversarial Tactics and Practical Defenses

The table below maps adversarial techniques to real-world examples and the defenses that hold up in practice.

Table 7.1: Adversarial techniques mapped to real-world examples and practical defenses. Chapter cross-references indicate where the defense is treated in depth.

Adversarial Technique	Real-World Example	Defense That Holds
Evasion (feature-space)	Malware padded with benign bytes to fool an ML classifier	Adversarial training, ensemble detection, hybrid AI + rules, behavioral monitoring post-execution
Evasion (content-level)	Phishing stripped to a vague availability request with no link or attachment	Policy-based risk scoring for context-free external messages, employee training on verification triggers
Evasion (slow-and-low)	Small-batch data exfiltration mimicking normal app traffic over weeks	Cumulative-volume alerts, behavioral baseline, cross-surface correlation (Ch 5)
Data poisoning (labels)	Compromised ticketing system flipping attack labels to benign before retraining	Restricted label authority, dataset anomaly validation, cross-verification before retraining

Adversarial Technique	Real-World Example	Defense That Holds
Data poisoning (backdoor)	Poisoned open-source model that misclassifies inputs with a trigger token	Model provenance, integrity checks, poisoning-signature testing, supply-chain discipline (Ch 4)
Model extraction	Systematic API querying to build an offline copy for evasion testing	Rate-limiting, query-pattern monitoring, output perturbation, and access controls on model endpoints
Training-data extraction	Prompt engineering that coaxes PII or internal details from an LLM	Minimize sensitive data in training, output filtering, red-team leakage testing (Ch 2)
Direct prompt injection	User input overriding system prompts to redirect agent behavior	Input sanitization, system/user context separation, HITL on state-changing tool calls
Indirect prompt injection	Malicious instructions hidden in a support ticket read by an investigation agent	Treat retrieved content as untrusted, MCP input filtering, scope agent tool access (Ch 6)
Deepfake impersonation	AI voice mimicking a CFO to authorize a wire transfer	Callback verification, multi-person approval, and retired voice-only approval paths
Autonomous offensive agent	Machine-speed vulnerability discovery and lateral movement during exercises	Patch discipline, runtime sensors (Ch 4), cross-surface correlation (Ch 5), continuous red-teaming (Ch 2)

Case Studies

Case Study 1: Attackers Adapting to an AI Email Filter

A company deployed an AI-based email security filter and saw early gains. Obvious phishing attempts with links and attachments dropped sharply, and the SOC reported fewer high-risk messages reaching inboxes.

Attackers adapted within weeks. They shifted to short, context-light emails that looked harmless in isolation—"Hi, are you available? I need a quick task,"—carrying neither a link nor a file, offering few features for the model to score. Employees replied, thinking the message came from an internal leader, and the attacker moved the conversation into a channel with weaker controls. In several attempts, the attacker shifted to SMS or a personal messaging platform after the first reply, reducing visibility entirely.

The defense lesson emerged quickly. The company updated the model and policy to treat vague availability emails from external domains as higher risk, trained staff to treat unexpected context-free requests as a verification trigger, and added a detection rule for conversations that moved to out-of-band channels immediately after first contact. The story illustrates the real pattern of adversarial work: AI defenses change attackers, defenders update both models and human processes, and the cycle continues.

Case Study 2: Adversarial Evasion Against a Malware Classifier

An organization relied on an ML-based malware classifier for early detection (the same class of system described in Chapter 2's case study, now viewed from the adversary's perspective). An attacker crafted a new malware variant specifically designed to pass the classifier.

The technique was straightforward. The attacker took a malicious payload and padded it with benign-looking byte sequences copied from common commercial software. The model's feature extraction picked up the added goodware signals and labeled the file as clean. The padded malware entered the environment undetected by the classifier.

Two safeguards, prepared in advance, caught the intrusion. First, endpoint detection and response observed suspicious post-execution behavior—process injection, credential access, and an unusual persistence mechanism—that the file-level classifier had missed. Second, network monitoring flagged command-and-control traffic to a newly registered domain. The combination of behavioral detection and network anomaly detection stopped the intrusion before lateral movement completed.

The incident became feedback for the classifier. The security team added the evasion sample and similar decoys to the retraining set, added pre-processing to reduce the influence of padding in feature extraction, and ran a controlled re-evaluation to confirm the improvement. The classifier became harder to trick through that specific technique. The broader lesson is that a single detection layer never covers full space, and disciplined post-incident retraining turns every evasion into a stronger future defense.

KPIs to Track

Metrics turn adversarial risk from a theoretical concern into operational work.

Adversarial probing detection. If an AI model is exposed through APIs or internal tools, measure anomalies in query patterns—repeated variants that look like boundary testing, systematic coverage of input space, and extraction-style sequential queries. A rising trend triggers rate-limit tightening and investigation.

Robustness assessment results. Use scheduled AI red-team exercises (Chapter 2) to measure how much perturbation causes misclassification, and track improvement over time. A model that resists more sophisticated adversarial inputs quarter over quarter is demonstrating operational resilience.

Deepfake and impersonation incidents. Track both successful and blocked attempts, segmented by channel (email, voice, video). Link incidents to process changes, such as callback verification adoption and retirement of voice-only approval paths.

Training data integrity. Track the percentage of training data sourced from trusted pipelines, the number of anomalies rejected during dataset preparation, and the cadence of validation checks. A program where one hundred percent of retraining data passes integrity checks is in a different class from one where validation is ad hoc.

Model drift monitoring. Maintain a drift index comparing current data distributions to training baselines. Treat drift thresholds as triggers for investigation—is the drift environmental (legitimate change) or adversarial (someone influencing the input distribution)?

Recovery time after AI incidents. If a model is compromised, poisoned, or proven weak against a new evasion technique, measure how quickly the team restores acceptable performance through retraining, patching, or rule updates. Recovery time is the ultimate test of lifecycle readiness.

Evasion-to-detection feedback velocity. When an evasion bypass is discovered, track how quickly the finding becomes an updated detection pattern, an adversarial training sample, or a new behavioral rule. Finding that takes months to flow back is adversarial debt. A finding that flows back within days is compound interest.

Risks and Guardrails

Complacency after initial AI deployment. When AI blocks common attacks, teams can assume the threat decreased. In reality, attackers changed tactics. The guardrail is threat intelligence, adversarial ML knowledge sharing, and periodic effectiveness reviews that include red-team probing specifically designed to test AI-driven controls.

AI infrastructure as an undefended target. AI frameworks, model-serving tools, and training pipelines have vulnerabilities and misconfigurations like any production stack. The guardrail is patching, network-access restriction, credential rotation, and monitoring the model's own health signals so sudden drops in alert volume or output-quality changes trigger investigation rather than relief.

Poisoned external data sources. Public threat feeds, open-source models, and community-contributed indicators can carry poisoning risk. The guardrail is vetting sources, cross-verifying across multiple feeds, and treating contributed data with the same skepticism applied to any untrusted input.

Model confidentiality erosion. A stolen model becomes an offline bypass-testing lab. Internal models can contain sensitive data fingerprints. The guardrail is restricted access, rate-limiting, extraction-pattern monitoring, output perturbation, and treating models as sensitive assets in the asset register and risk framework.

Removing defense-in-depth because AI is present. Teams that trust AI detection alone and decommission older layers create a single point of failure that the adversary only needs to beat once. The guardrail is preserving layered detection—AI, rules, behavioral analytics, deception, and human review—especially for controls that catch post-execution behavior.

Legal and reputational risk from AI-enabled fraud. When a deepfake or an AI-driven attack succeeds, the organization faces not only financial loss but questions about whether its controls were adequate. The guardrail is documenting adversarial testing, maintaining audit trails for model changes and policy decisions, and building response plans that treat AI-enabled incidents with the same severity as any other high-impact security event.

Executive Takeaways

- **Adversarial AI operates on three layers simultaneously.** Attackers weaponize AI, evade AI defenses, and target AI systems directly. Defensive planning that treats only one layer as "the problem" misses two-thirds of the risk.
- **Evasion is the natural successor to every detection improvement.** Every AI detection boundary has exploitable margins. Defense-in-depth—AI, rules, behavior, deception, human verification—means the attacker must beat multiple independent systems.
- **Poisoning targets the learning pipeline, not the running model.** Restrict who can influence training data, validate datasets before retraining, and treat model updates with the same release discipline as production software.
- **Prompt injection scales with agent scope.** The more tools, credentials, and data an agent can reach, the larger the blast radius of a successful injection. Least-privilege scoping, input sanitization, and HITL on destructive actions are the controls.

- **Retire voice-only approval paths for sensitive actions.** Deepfakes target trust. Process controls—callback verification, multi-person approval, contextual challenges—reduce risk more reliably than human intuition under pressure.
- **Autonomous offensive agents compress surprise windows.** Patch discipline, runtime sensors, cross-surface correlation, and continuous red-teaming keep defenders adapting at a pace that matches the adversary.
- **Defend the AI lifecycle: build, deploy, operate.** Secure training data, harden deployment, monitor drift, red team continuously, and retrain through controlled releases. A lifecycle view prevents the "buy and forget" habit that adversaries exploit.
- **Turn every evasion into a stronger future defense.** Post-incident retraining, adversarial sample injection, and detection-logic updates close the feedback loop. The organizations that compound learning hold the edge.

End-of-Chapter Reflection Questions

- For each AI-driven detection system in your environment, when was the last time a red team specifically tested it with adversarial inputs? What did the exercise reveal about the model's boundaries?
- If an attacker queried your model API systematically for a week, would your monitoring detect the extraction attempt? How quickly would the alert reach a human?
- Which of your AI systems retrain on their own outputs, and what controls prevent feedback-loop pollution from adversarial samples?
- Map each of the eleven adversarial techniques in Table 7.1 to a control you already have, a control you are building, or a gap. Which gap carries the highest business risk?
- If a deepfake voice impersonated your CEO and requested an urgent wire transfer today, which process control would stop it? Has that control been tested with a realistic simulation?
- For every model or agent exposed through an API or MCP connection, can you state who has access, what rate limits apply, and what monitoring exists for extraction or abuse patterns?
- How quickly does a discovered evasion bypass become an updated detection pattern in your environment? Is feedback instrumented, or does it depend on manual effort?
- If a poisoned model or adapter were introduced into your supply chain tomorrow, which control would catch it before it reached production? How was that control last tested?

Chapter 8

ETHICS, PRIVACY, AND REGULATORY COMPLIANCE

Trust Turns into a Security Control

Security teams collect signals, connect patterns, and respond fast. Legal teams define purpose, reduce exposure, and document decisions. Product teams keep friction proportional to value. AI brings these instincts into the same room because it sits inside security workflows and influences outcomes that affect people directly—whether the person is an employee trying to do their job, a customer trying to complete a transaction, or a data principal whose records move through an AI pipeline they never consented to.

This chapter treats ethics, privacy, and regulatory compliance as core parts of security effectiveness, not as overhead. A privacy-first design keeps the organization credible and also improves signal quality because the data has a clear purpose and a clear handling path. A fairness-first approach reduces friction spikes across regions and roles, keeping people willing to cooperate with investigations. Strong documentation and audit trails satisfy regulators and also help engineering and SOC teams tune systems responsibly. And automated governance—GRC agents integrated with live systems, pulling evidence continuously rather than assembling it under audit pressure—turns compliance from a periodic scramble into a steady-state operation.

The goal for a leader stays practical: applying AI in a way that produces measurable protection, respects people, holds up under scrutiny from any jurisdiction, and generates the evidence to prove it.

The Regulatory and Framework Landscape

The regulatory environment around AI has matured from advisory to enforceable. Leaders who treat compliance as a map rather than a burden find that the frameworks converge more than they diverge, and that building once to the strictest applicable standard simplifies operations. The table below summarizes the landscape.

Table 8.1: The regulatory and framework landscape for AI-in-security programs. Build once to the strictest applicable standard; map to the others.

Framework / Regulation	Scope	What It Demands of AI-in-Security Programs
EU AI Act	Risk-tiered obligations for AI across the EU; affects any org serving EU residents	Prohibited practices, high-risk system requirements (transparency, logging, human oversight, risk management), conformity assessments, post-market monitoring, AI literacy
GDPR	Personal data processing in the EU and for EU data subjects	Lawful basis, purpose limitation, data minimization, DPIA for high-risk processing, automated decision-making rights (Art. 22), breach notification within 72 hours
India DPDPA	Personal data of Indian data principals	Consent-based processing, purpose limitation, retention minimization, breach notification, data principal rights, data fiduciary obligations, cross-border transfer restrictions
NIST AI RMF	Voluntary US framework for managing AI risk	Govern, Map, Measure, Manage functions; risk identification, impact assessment, monitoring, and documentation; widely used as a reference even outside the US
ISO/IEC 42001	Certifiable AI management system	AIMS (AI Management System): AI policy, risk assessment, objectives, controls, operational planning, performance evaluation, continual improvement; Annex A control objectives covering AI lifecycle
ISO/IEC 27001 / 27701	Information security and privacy management	ISMS and PIMS controls applied to AI data flows; certification demonstrates security and privacy governance discipline
NIST CSF 2.0	Cybersecurity risk management (US, widely adopted globally)	Govern, Identify, Protect, Detect, Respond, Recover functions applied to AI-assisted security systems
OECD AI Principles	Principles-based intergovernmental guidance	Transparency, explainability, accountability, fairness, robustness, and safety; referenced by many national frameworks

Framework / Regulation	Scope	What It Demands of AI-in-Security Programs
SEC Cyber Disclosure	US public companies	Material incident disclosure within four business days raises the stakes on detection and investigation speed for AI-SOC
DORA (EU)	Financial services operational resilience	ICT risk management, incident reporting, third-party risk (including AI vendors), resilience testing
HIPAA	Protected health information (US healthcare)	Security and privacy of PHI when processed by AI systems; applies to AI analytics on patient data
PCI DSS 4.0	Payment card data	Security controls on AI systems that touch cardholder data: logging, access controls, vulnerability management

ISO/IEC 42001: The AI Management System in Practice

ISO/IEC 42001 is the first certifiable management system standard specifically for AI. It follows the Annex SL structure familiar from ISO 27001, which means organizations already running an ISMS can extend their management system to cover AI without starting from scratch. The standard is structured around seven core clauses and an Annex A of control objectives.

What it requires. An AI policy approved by leadership. An AI risk assessment that identifies risks from the AI system's design, data, deployment, and operation. Documented objectives for responsible AI use. Operational planning and controls covering the AI lifecycle—from data collection and model training through deployment, monitoring, and retirement. Internal audit and management review. Continual improvement based on monitoring, incidents, and stakeholder feedback.

How it maps to security AI. For a security program deploying AI-driven detection, response, or governance, ISO 42001 translates into practical requirements. Every AI system that influences a security decision needs an entry in the AI inventory with a documented owner, risk classification, data sources, and human-oversight boundaries. Every model update follows a controlled release process. Post-deployment monitoring covers drift, bias, and performance degradation. Incident management covers AI-specific failures—poisoning, evasion bypass, agent compromise—alongside traditional security incidents.

Certification value. Certification demonstrates to regulators, customers, and partners that the organization manages AI risk through a repeatable, auditable system rather than ad hoc judgment. For organizations already ISO 27001 certified, adding 42001 is an incremental effort that produces disproportionate credibility. For organizations subject to the EU AI Act, ISO 42001 alignment covers a significant share of the Act's governance expectations, simplifying conformity assessment work.

Sub-Processor Due Diligence: Onboarding AI Tools and SaaS

Every AI tool or SaaS application that processes organizational data introduces a sub-processor relationship. Under GDPR, DPDPA, and most modern privacy frameworks, the data controller (or data fiduciary) remains accountable for what the sub-processor does with the data. Due diligence at onboarding is not optional; it is a regulatory obligation with direct liability consequences.

What to Evaluate Before Onboarding

Data processing scope and purpose. What data does the tool access? Does it process content (email bodies, code, documents) or only metadata? Does it use customer data for its own model training by default? Consumer-tier AI services often retain and train on inputs unless enterprise terms are negotiated. An engineer pasting source code into a consumer AI assistant is creating a sub-processor relationship the legal team has not reviewed.

Data residency and geolocation requirements. Where is the data processed, and where is it stored? DPDPA restricts cross-border transfers of personal data to jurisdictions or entities that meet specified conditions. GDPR requires adequate safeguards for transfers outside the EEA. Many sector regulations (banking, healthcare, government) add jurisdiction-specific residency requirements. A cloud-hosted AI service that routes prompts through a US data center may violate Indian residency expectations for a product serving Indian data principals. The evaluation must cover not only the primary service but also every downstream service the tool calls—inference APIs, vector databases, logging infrastructure, and backup storage.

Sub-processor chain. Does the vendor use its own sub-processors? A SaaS AI tool that sends data to a third-party model provider, a vector-database service, and a monitoring platform creates a chain of sub-processors, each with its own data handling, retention, and jurisdiction. The onboarding evaluation must map the full chain, not just the first hop. GDPR Article 28 and DPDPA both impose obligations on this chain.

Retention and deletion. How long does the vendor retain data, prompts, and model outputs? What happens at contract termination? Can you verify deletion? A vendor that retains prompt logs indefinitely or cannot demonstrate deletion on request creates ongoing liability.

Security posture. What certifications does the vendor hold (ISO 27001, SOC 2 Type II, ISO 42001)? What incident notification timeline does the contract specify? Is there a right to audit? Does the vendor's security posture cover the AI-specific risks from Chapter 7—prompt injection defense, model supply-chain integrity, agent scope controls?

Contractual protection. Data processing agreements (DPAs) must specify purpose, scope, retention, deletion, sub-processor approval, breach notification, and audit rights. For AI-specific tools, add clauses covering: no training on customer data without explicit consent, zero-retention processing options, model versioning and rollback capabilities, and liability for AI-specific failures.

A practical example makes this concrete. A security team evaluates an AI-powered threat intelligence platform. The platform ingests in IOCs, enriches alerts, and produces summaries. During due diligence, the team discovers that the platform sends alert data to a US-based inference API, stores enriched outputs in a vector database hosted in Ireland, and retains all prompts for ninety days for "quality improvement." The team's Indian operations serve data principals under DPDPA, and the cross-border transfer to the US inference API lacks the contractual safeguards DPDPA requires. The onboarding is paused until the vendor offers a single-region deployment option and updates the DPA to include explicit processing restrictions, zero-retention on prompts, and breach notification within the timeline DPDPA mandates. This is due diligence operating as it should—before the data moves, not after.

GRC Agents: Continuous Compliance From Live Evidence

Traditional GRC operates on a cadence—quarterly risk assessments, annual audits, periodic control testing. The gap between assessments is where drift accumulates, controls degrade, and evidence goes stale. AI-powered GRC agents change this model by integrating directly with the systems they govern and pulling evidence continuously.

What a GRC agent does. A GRC agent connects to the organization's control environment—identity provider, SIEM, cloud posture tools, CI/CD pipelines, AI inventory, SaaS security platforms, data classification systems—and continuously evaluates whether controls are operating as designed. When a control deviates from its defined state, the agent generates an evidence-backed finding in real time, not at the next audit cycle.

Example: ISO 42001 control monitoring. ISO 42001 requires post-deployment monitoring for AI systems. A GRC agent connected to the AI inventory and the model-monitoring platform can continuously verify that every deployed AI system has active drift monitoring, that the monitoring has not been silently disabled, that alert thresholds have not been changed without documented approval, and that the last evaluation date falls within the policy window.

A deviation—a model running in production for six months without evaluation—surfaces as a finding the same day, not at the next internal audit.

Example: Data residency compliance. A GRC agent connected to cloud infrastructure and SaaS platforms monitors where data is processed and stored. When a new SaaS integration routes data through a jurisdiction that conflicts with the organization's residency policy, the agent flags the deviation with the relevant contractual and regulatory reference. The GRC team reviews and either approves with documented justification or blocks the integration before data moves.

Example: Sub-processor chain validation. A GRC agent maintains a live map of sub-processor relationships. When a vendor adds a new sub-processor—which GDPR Article 28 requires notification of—the agent detects the change through contract-monitoring feeds or vendor notification channels and triggers a review workflow. The review includes data-flow analysis, jurisdiction check, and DPA adequacy assessment. Without the agent, the notification sits in a legal inbox until someone reads it; with the agent, the review starts within hours.

The operational pattern is the same across all three examples. The GRC agent replaces periodic human evidence collection with continuous machine evidence collection, reduces the window between control failure and detection from months to hours, and produces audit-ready evidence as a by-product of daily operations rather than as a special project. Organizations that deploy GRC agents report audit preparation times dropping from weeks to days, because the evidence already exists, is already structured, and is already linked to the control framework.

Ethics, Fairness, and Human Oversight

Data Minimization with Security Intent

Security teams often feel pressure to collect every possible signal because more data can improve detection. Privacy rules and trust expectations push a different discipline: collect what supports the stated purpose, limit secondary use, control retention, and protect access. A practical method begins with a data map—what signals feed the model, where each signal comes from, how long each is retained, and who can access raw data, derived features, and model outputs. Once the map exists, teams can make purposeful cuts. For phishing detection, many systems can focus on sender reputation, headers, URLs, and behavioral patterns while leaving message body content outside the default pipeline. For anomaly detection, pseudonymized identifiers support modeling, and a controlled process maps a flagged identifier back to a person only when a case crosses a defined threshold.

Retention limits provide both legal and operational value. Behavior profiles stored indefinitely increase exposure and create a surveillance perception. A defined retention window aligned to investigation needs reduces exposure, makes communication easier, and limits blast radius during a breach. Minimization also supports a clean story—leaders can explain what data the system uses, why those signals matter, and how the organization protects that data. That clarity reduces anxiety and resistance.

Fairness, Bias, and Disparity as Quality Control

Bias in security AI often emerges through proxies. A model uses IP reputation, location, or device patterns to infer risk, and those signals correlate with geography, socioeconomic factors, and work style. A model that flags certain regions disproportionately creates friction for legitimate users, increases support volume, and harms trust—outcomes that lower security posture because frustrated users route around controls.

Subgroup testing is the simplest control. Compare false positive and false negative rates across roles, departments, and geographies that reflect real operational differences. Investigate drivers. Sometimes the disparity has a valid explanation (travel-heavy roles). Sometimes it reflects a weak proxy (IP-based scoring penalizes remote workers in specific countries). Mitigation includes feature adjustments, threshold tuning per cohort, improved training data diversity, and human review for segments where uncertainty stays high. The key output for leadership is evidence: proof that teams measured disparity, tuned the system, and kept monitoring.

Human Oversight and Contestability

Regulatory frameworks consistently emphasize human oversight when outcomes materially affect people. In security, that requirement becomes a control rather than a burden. AI surfaces risk and recommends actions. Humans own outcomes—termination recommendations, disciplinary actions, and long-term access restrictions. For customer-facing controls, AI triggers temporary step-up checks or short holds, while the organization maintains a clear path for review and reversal. GDPR Article 22 gives data subjects the right not to be subject to a decision based solely on automated processing that produces legal or similarly significant effects. The EU AI Act reinforces this for high-risk systems. DPDPA provides data principals with the right to access information about significant decisions and the logic involved. Operationally, this means structured decision logging, a defined appeal process, and fast reversal mechanisms.

Structured Decision Logging: The Audit Trail That Works

A vague record creates confusion for support teams, auditors, and affected users. A structured decision trail connects action to signals and policy. A sample log entry: "Account Alice disabled at 10:43. Trigger signals: login from two countries within one hour and five failed password attempts.

Risk score 98, high. Action taken per incident response runbook INF-1. Reviewer: SOC lead. Re-enable permitted after identity verification." This style of logging supports three outcomes at once. The user can understand the rationale and request a review. An auditor can see that the decision relied on security signals rather than personal characteristics. The security team can analyze aggregate trends and tune thresholds. When the account is re-enabled, the trail records the safeguard, including time stamp, reviewer, and reversal reason. Over time, the organization gains a dataset that improves both model tuning and policy design.

Case Study: Employee Monitoring AI Under GDPR and DPDPA Pressure

A multinational company with operations in Europe and India rolled out an AI system for insider threat detection by analyzing device usage patterns and communication signals. The initial design processed full message content and attempted broad behavioral scoring beyond a narrow security purpose. Employees and works councils raised concerns, and the organization faced risk under GDPR and labor rules due to broad monitoring, weak purpose justification, and limited safeguards. In India, the same system processed personal data of Indian employees without a documented lawful basis under DPDPA, and the cross-border transfer of behavioral data to a centralized European platform lacked the contractual protections DPDPA requires.

The company reworked the deployment across both jurisdictions. It narrowed the data scope to security-relevant metadata and event signals. It documented the lawful basis for processing under both GDPR (legitimate interest with DPIA) and DPDPA (consent with clear purpose statement). It reduced intrusiveness, clarified purpose and permitted uses in policy, introduced oversight through a defined review path, and issued a transparency memo describing data scope, purpose, retention, access rules, and safeguards. Managers received guidance that security signals serve investigations rather than judgment. For Indian employees, the processing was localized to a regional instance to meet residency expectations, and the DPA with the European platform was updated to cover AI-specific processing restrictions.

The revised system surfaced a real incident—abnormal activity consistent with an attempted customer-data exfiltration. A human investigation team validated evidence, followed established HR and legal processes, and took action with documentation and review. The organization improved its security posture, reduced legal exposure, preserved employee trust across both jurisdictions, and kept the program viable long-term.

The leadership lesson: capability alone never justifies use. Targeted, lawful AI use scales better, creates fewer internal battles, and survives audits in every jurisdiction the organization operates in.

KPIs to Track

DPIA and AI impact assessment coverage. Track completion and sign-off for assessments on all AI systems involving personal data, with full coverage as the target. A program where new AI deployments are launched without assessment is a program waiting for a regulatory finding.

Bias and disparity audit results. Track false positive rates by region, role, and department alongside audit cadence and remediation completion. Evidence of measurement, action, and follow-through is what auditors and regulators look for.

Sub-processor due diligence completion. Track the percentage of AI tools and SaaS applications with completed due diligence before data processing begins. Measure time from vendor selection to DPA execution. A program that processes data before due diligence is complete is operating with unmanaged liability.

Data residency compliance. Track the percentage of AI data flows compliant with jurisdiction-specific residency requirements. Deviations surface through GRC agent monitoring and are remediated before audit, not during.

GRC agent coverage and finding velocity. Track the percentage of AI controls monitored by GRC agents, the mean time from control deviation to finding generation, and the mean time from finding to remediation. Coverage above eighty percent and finding-to-remediation under seven days are meaningful milestones.

Trust and friction indicators. Track complaint volume, appeal counts, support tickets linked to AI controls, and survey-based trust indicators. For workforce contexts, including sentiment signals and escalations mentioning monitoring concerns.

Regulatory findings. Track audit outcomes with a target of zero major findings tied to AI documentation, transparency, or data handling.

Governance process adherence. Track the percentage of AI projects reviewed through the required checklist, documented in inventory, risk-classified, and assigned clear owners. Full adherence is the target; gaps are findings.

Risks and Guardrails

Regulatory exposure. AI deployments without privacy and legal review can lead to fines, mandatory changes, or processing bans. The guardrail involves privacy and legal teams early, completing impact assessments, and assigning an owner for tracking regulatory changes across every jurisdiction the organization operates in.

Sub-processor chain liability. A vendor's downstream sub-processor mishandles data, and the organization is accountable. The guardrail is full chain mapping, contractual flow-down of obligations, right to audit, and GRC agent monitoring that detects sub-processor changes in near real time.

Geolocation non-compliance. Data routed through a jurisdiction that conflicts with residency requirements creates immediate regulatory risk. The guardrail is infrastructure-level controls (region-locked deployments, egress restrictions) combined with continuous GRC agent monitoring of data-flow paths.

Backlash and loss of trust. Lawful systems can still face backlash when perceived as surveillance. The guardrail is transparency, purpose clarity, and alignment with user interests—communicated before deployment, not after complaints.

Scope creep and secondary use. Signals collected for security become attractive for HR analytics, productivity monitoring, or marketing. The guardrail is a permitted-use policy, access restrictions, and approval requirements for any use beyond the documented security purpose.

Stale evidence and audit gaps. Annual evidence collection creates a window where controls may have failed without documentation. The guardrail is GRC agent integration that produces continuous evidence, replacing periodic collection with steady-state monitoring.

Executive Takeaways

- **The regulatory landscape has converged around accountability.** EU AI Act, GDPR, DPDPA, NIST AI RMF, ISO 42001, and sector rules all demand documented risk management, human oversight, transparency, and post-deployment monitoring. Build once to the strictest standard; map to the rest.
- **ISO 42001 is the management-system anchor.** For organizations already running ISO 27001, extending to 42001 is incremental. For organizations subject to the EU AI Act, 42001 alignment covers a significant share of governance expectations.
- **Sub-processor due diligence is a regulatory obligation, not a courtesy.** Map the full chain, evaluate residency, negotiate AI-specific DPA clauses, and verify before data moves—not after.
- **Geolocation compliance is a design constraint, not a post-deployment fix.** Where data is processed and stored must be determined during architecture, locked in infrastructure, and monitored continuously.

- **GRC agents replace periodic scrambles with continuous evidence.** Integrate with live systems, pull control-state evidence continuously, and generate audit-ready artifacts as a by-product of daily operations.
- **Ethics and fairness are quality controls, not abstract principles.** Measure disparity, tune for fairness, maintain human oversight on consequential decisions, and produce the evidence that demonstrates all three.
- **Structured decision logging is the audit trail that works.** Connect every AI-driven action to trigger signals, risk score, policy reference, reviewer, and reversal path. The trail supports the user, the auditor, and the tuning team simultaneously.
- **Governance is product work.** Treat it as something the system produces automatically, not as something humans assemble under pressure. The organizations that embed governance into daily operations are the ones that survive scrutiny in every jurisdiction.

End-of-Chapter Reflection Questions

- For every AI system that influences a security decision in your organization, is there a completed impact assessment, a documented owner, a risk classification, and a defined human-oversight boundary? Where are the blanks?
- When was the last time your organization onboarded a new AI tool or SaaS application that processes personal data? Was a full sub-processor due diligence completed before data processing began, or after?
- Can you produce, within an hour, a map of every jurisdiction where AI systems in your security program process personal data, and the legal basis for processing in each?
- If a GRC agent were connected to your AI inventory and model-monitoring platform today, what percentage of deployed AI systems would it find with active post-deployment monitoring? What would the deviation report look like?
- For your highest-impact AI-driven security action—account lockout, transaction block, access revocation—does the decision log contain the trigger signals, risk score, policy reference, reviewer, and reversal path? Could a regulator reconstruct the decision from the log alone?
- How does your organization ensure that signals collected for security are not repurposed for HR analytics, productivity monitoring, or other secondary uses? Is the boundary a policy, a technical control, or both?

- If a vendor you use for AI-powered security added a new sub-processor tomorrow, how quickly would your GRC team know, and what process would trigger?
- For the AI systems serving data principals in India, can you demonstrate DPDPA-compliant consent, purpose limitation, retention minimization, and breach notification readiness? Where is the evidence produced—automatically, or by hand?

Chapter 9

THE ROAD AHEAD–QUANTUM, SOVEREIGN AI, AND THE EVOLVING SECURITY LANDSCAPE

The Next Few Years Will Feel Faster and Wider

Security leaders have watched technology waves stack up. The coming phase adds a combination that pushes pace and surface area upward together. Quantum computing places current cryptography on a long-term clock. Sovereign AI strategies reshape where models, data, and compute are permitted to live. Edge AI and cyber-physical convergence extend the security perimeter into factories, vehicles, and critical infrastructure, where compromise creates physical consequences. And the security workforce itself is being reshaped by the tools it operates, with roles evolving faster than most training programs can keep pace with.

A workable plan avoids two traps. One trap treats these trends as distant and theoretical, so planning never begins. The other treats every new topic as urgent, so teams chase hype and create complexity. Practical readiness sits in the middle: keep fundamentals strong, test new capabilities in controlled ways, and build a few capabilities that reduce surprise. This chapter provides the planning anchors—what to start now, what to watch, and what to treat as a longer investment with clear ownership and measurable progress.

Quantum Readiness and Post-Quantum Migration

Public-key cryptography underpins trust across modern digital systems. RSA and elliptic-curve cryptography support key exchange, digital signatures, certificates, secure web traffic, VPN tunnels, and identity systems. Quantum computing matters because a sufficiently capable quantum computer can solve the mathematical problems behind these algorithms efficiently, undermining the security assumptions that protect them.

Timing remains uncertain, but planning has urgency for two reasons. First, the collect-now-decrypt-later pattern creates immediate risk for data with long confidentiality needs—health records, intellectual property, financial records, government-linked information. Adversaries recording encrypted traffic today can decrypt it when quantum capability arrives. Second, migrations take time even when standards exist, because cryptography sits inside applications, libraries, certificates, hardware devices, vendor services, and legacy platforms. Quantum readiness behaves like a multi-year operational program, not a patch cycle.

Crypto Agility as the Practical Starting Point

Quantum readiness becomes actionable when leaders ask a near-term question: how quickly can the organization change cryptography across its environment without breaking production? Crypto agility means the organization can inventory where vulnerable algorithms sit, replace them through controlled releases, manage certificates and keys at scale, and keep evidence of testing and rollouts.

Start with an inventory that goes beyond a checklist. Map where RSA and ECC appear across internal PKI, certificate authorities, VPN tunnels, remote access, APIs, code signing, key wrapping, and hardware security modules. Record ownership, upgrade paths, and dependencies—especially where embedded devices or legacy systems depend on older libraries. Include shadow crypto and one-off implementations that hide in automation scripts and vendor integrations.

Phase work by risk and feasibility. Prioritize systems protecting long-lived sensitive data first. Move external-facing connections toward hybrid approaches where classical and post-quantum methods operate together during transition. Use test environments that mirror production to evaluate handshake timing, certificate size implications, and client compatibility. Scale rollouts with clear guardrails and rollback plans.

Case Study: Crypto Inventory at a Global Bank

A global bank initiated its post-quantum readiness program with a crypto inventory audit. The discovery phase, supported by automated scanning across certificate stores, code repositories, infrastructure configurations, and vendor integration points, identified over twelve thousand cryptographic dependencies. Roughly thirty percent were in systems the security team had not previously cataloged—internal automation scripts using hardcoded key exchanges, vendor-managed HSMs with firmware-locked algorithms, and legacy payment gateways using RSA-1024 that predated the current architecture.

The inventory became the migration roadmap. Systems were categorized into three tiers: immediate candidates for hybrid classical-plus-PQC migration (external-facing APIs and certificate infrastructure), medium-term candidates requiring vendor coordination (payment gateways, partner integrations), and long-term candidates requiring hardware replacement (embedded HSMs, legacy terminals). The program set quarterly milestones and reported progress to the board alongside other operational resilience metrics. The crypto agility built during this program paid an unplanned dividend six months later when a non-quantum cryptographic vulnerability required rapid certificate rotation across the same estate—a rotation that completed in days rather than the weeks it would have taken without the inventory and tooling.

Sovereign AI and Data Sovereignty

Sovereign AI refers to the growing trend of nations and regions asserting control over AI infrastructure—compute, models, training data, and rules governing their use. For security leaders, sovereign AI is not a geopolitical abstraction. It is a set of constraints that directly affects where AI systems can run, which models can be used, where data can be processed, and what governance obligations apply.

National AI strategies and computing sovereignty. Several countries and blocs are investing in domestic AI computing infrastructure, establishing national model registries, and restricting the export or import of certain AI capabilities. For a multinational security program, this means the AI tools available in one jurisdiction may not be available or permissible in another. A threat-detection model trained on data from one region may face restrictions on deployment in another. A cloud-hosted AI service that routes inference through a US data center may be incompatible with data-sovereignty requirements in India, the EU, or the Gulf.

Model access restrictions and export controls. Export controls on advanced AI chips and models are tightening. Security teams that depend on frontier models accessed through cloud APIs face a planning question: what happens if access to a specific model is restricted, rate-limited, or withdrawn in a specific jurisdiction? Programs that build on a single provider's model without an alternative create a concentration risk that is both operational and geopolitical.

Implications for security architecture. The practical response is architecture that accommodates sovereignty constraints by design rather than as a post-deployment fix. Region-locked deployments for sensitive workloads. Multi-model strategies that include open-weight models deployable on sovereign infrastructure alongside frontier models for less-sensitive tasks. Data-flow mapping (Chapter 8's sub-processor due diligence) extended to cover model provenance and inference jurisdiction. And governance that can demonstrate compliance with the local AI framework—whether that is the EU AI Act, India's evolving AI governance, or sector-specific rules—in each jurisdiction the program operates in.

Sovereign AI is a slow-moving force with compounding impact. Organizations that build flexibility into their architecture now will adapt smoothly as requirements evolve. Organizations that build on a single-jurisdiction assumption will face expensive re-architecture later.

Edge AI and Cyber-Physical Convergence

As connectivity expands through 5G and its successors, more devices run local models to make decisions close to sensors and machines—in factories, vehicles, smart grids, logistics fleets, medical devices, and critical infrastructure. This expands the threat surface because each connected device becomes an endpoint with its own software supply chain, update mechanism, and identity. Compromise can create physical impact, operational disruption, and safety consequences that no pure IT incident produces.

Device identity and model integrity. Edge AI turns devices into decision-makers, and decision-makers need trustworthy identity and trusted updates. Secure boot, signed firmware, certificate-based onboarding, and revocation procedures for fleets are foundational. Model integrity controls—signed model artifacts, version verification, and tamper detection—prevent an attacker from replacing the model running on a device with a poisoned version that produces unsafe outputs while appearing to function normally.

Monitoring at scale. Humans cannot interpret telemetry from thousands of edge devices producing noisy signals in mixed formats. AI-based monitoring becomes necessary—creating a dual requirement: protect edge AI from tampering and use AI to monitor edge behavior at scale. Anomaly detection on OT protocols, multimodal correlation of cyber and physical signals, and fleet-level behavioral baselines are the techniques that work. The signals feed into the AI-SOC (Chapter 5) for correlation with enterprise telemetry.

Response design for safety-critical environments. A containment action that works well for an office laptop—isolate, reimage, restore—can cause operational shutdown or safety hazards in an industrial environment. Security teams need response tiers designed with operations leaders, so safety and continuity remain protected during fast incidents. The HITL framework from Chapter 1 applies with higher stakes: destructive actions on OT systems always require human approval from someone who understands the physical process, not just the cyber risk.

AI and the Future of Security Talent

AI is reshaping the security workforce in ways that are already visible but not yet fully absorbed into hiring, training, and career development.

Roles are evolving, not disappearing. The SOC analyst role is shifting from manual evidence assembly to AI-assisted investigation supervision—evaluating AI-generated case narratives, approving or overriding recommendations, and handling the incidents that AI cannot resolve autonomously. Detection engineering is splitting into two tracks: one focused on traditional rules and signature writing, and another focused on ML model evaluation, prompt engineering for security assistants, and adversarial-resilience testing. GRC analysts are becoming GRC agent operators (Chapter 8), configuring, tuning, and supervising automated compliance monitoring rather than assembling evidence by hand.

New skills are becoming essential. AI evaluation—understanding precision, recall, drift, and adversarial robustness—is no longer a data-science luxury; it is an operational skill every security team needs. Prompt engineering for security-specific use cases matters because the quality of AI-assisted investigation, code review, and threat hunting depends on how well the human frames the task. Agent governance—understanding tool scoping, MCP configuration, non-human identity management, and HITL placement—is the skill that prevents agentic AI from becoming an unmanaged risk surface.

The talent pipeline needs deliberate investment. Security skills shortages are concentrated in the specializations AI creates demand for: cloud security, AI/ML security, identity engineering, and detection engineering. Organizations that invest in internal training, rotation programs, and structured mentorship build capability faster than organizations that rely solely on external hiring. AI itself helps here—AI-assisted onboarding, simulation-based training, and copilot tools that let junior analysts operate at a higher level while they learn—but the investment in people has to be intentional, budgeted, and tracked.

The honest summary is that AI does not reduce the need for security professionals. It changes what security professionals need to know, raises the floor of what a junior can accomplish with good tools, and raises the ceiling of what a senior can accomplish with AI-powered leverage. Organizations that treat this as a workforce-development question, not just a technology question, will hold talent advantage.

Planning Anchors: What to Start, Watch, and Invest In

The table below provides a practical framework for categorizing future-facing security work. The categories are not rigid; items move from "watch" to "start" as standards mature and evidence accumulates.

Table 9.1: Planning anchors for future-facing security work. Items move from "Watch" to "Start" as standards and evidence mature.

Category	Start Now	Watch and Prepare	Invest for the Long Term
Quantum / PQC	Crypto inventory audit; hybrid PQC on external-facing connections	Vendor PQC roadmaps; hardware replacement planning for locked-algorithm devices	Full PKI migration; quantum-resistant key management across estate
Sovereign AI	Multi-model strategy; data-flow mapping by jurisdiction; region-locked sensitive deployments	National AI registry requirements; export-control developments	Sovereign compute infrastructure; jurisdiction-specific model fine-tuning
Edge / Cyber-Physical	Device identity discipline; model integrity controls for current fleets	5G/6G security implications; autonomous-system safety standards	Fleet-scale AI monitoring; OT-specific response automation
Talent	AI evaluation and prompt engineering training for existing staff; agent governance skills	Role evolution tracking; career-path redesign for AI-augmented security	Internal rotation programs; AI-powered training and onboarding at scale

KPIs to Track

Crypto agility and PQC progress. Track the percentage of external-facing connections protected through hybrid PQC methods. Track internal PKI and VPN transition progress. Keep exceptions documented with owners and timelines. Review quarterly.

Sovereign AI compliance. Track the percentage of AI deployments compliant with jurisdiction-specific data-sovereignty and model-governance requirements. Deviations surface through GRC agent monitoring (Chapter 8).

Edge and OT coverage. Track the percentage of edge/OT devices with certified identity, signed firmware, and active behavioral monitoring. Track incidents involving IoT or OT compromise and measure detection and containment performance.

Talent readiness. Track the percentage of security staff trained in AI evaluation, prompt engineering, and agent governance. Track internal capability across the critical specializations: cloud security, AI/ML security, identity engineering, and detection engineering. Growth over time reduces concentration risk.

Chapter 10

THE 6-SYSTEM OPERATING MODEL–FROM PILOT TO SCALE

Why Pilots Fade and Programs Stall

AI security programs often begin with energy and end with drift. A team buys a tool, runs a pilot, and gets early wins. Then the work stalls when production reality shows up. Alerts keep flowing, ownership stays fuzzy, data feeds break in small ways that compound over time, and governance arrives late—usually triggered by an audit request or an incident review that demands evidence the team never captured.

The pattern is consistent across industries. The technology may be strong while the program mechanics stay weak. A repeatable operating model prevents the slide by turning AI adoption into a program that runs week after week, regardless of vendor changes, headcount changes, or leadership transitions. The model here has six connected systems that run as a loop: Outcomes and Scope, Data Readiness, Phased Deployment, Measurable Performance, Governance and Guardrails, and Continuous Improvement. Each system produces artifacts that feed the next, creating momentum through cadence rather than heroics.

The Six Systems

System 1: Outcomes and Scope

Start by writing three outcome statements with clear owners. An outcome without an owner becomes a slogan. Pick two high-impact use cases—email/BEC correlation and identity triage tend to show value quickly because signal volume is high and correlation reduces duplicates. Define automation safety tiers (Chapter 1's HITL framework applied operationally): notify-only, low-risk auto, human-confirm, and break-glass. Capture baselines for MTTD, MTTR, false positive rate, and root-cause clarity from real work. The purpose is not perfection. The purpose is truth, so future movement becomes visible.

System 2: Data Readiness and Integration

AI output quality follows data quality. Build a crown-jewel asset map with owners and escalation paths. Normalize identifiers and timestamps across email, endpoint, identity, and cloud—many AI and correlation failures trace back to misalignment rather than model issues. Deploy missing-feed monitoring and schema-drift alerts with clear escalation owners. Define data contracts for critical feeds: what "healthy" looks like, who owns the feed, and what triggers when health slips. Target ninety-five percent coverage for the crown jewels. Broken-feed days above three per month create a fragile pipeline that will produce operational surprises.

System 3: Phased Deployment

Phased deployment reduces risk by controlling how AI moves from insight to action, and it builds trust by proving reliability before enabling automation. The sequence is predictable: shadow mode first (AI produces findings, humans decide), assisted workflows next (AI recommends, humans confirm), then carefully chosen low-blast-radius automation with rollback rehearsed. Tag every candidate procedure by blast radius and reversibility. Pair the catalog with an approval matrix that maps safety tiers to approvers. Practice rollback before rollout—a rollback that only exists on paper behaves poorly under pressure. A reversal rate under two percent indicates good threshold tuning; above five percent signals automation behaving as a liability.

System 4: Measurable Performance

KPI cards remove debate. Each case gets a card defining metrics, formulas, owners, and data sources. Dashboards are validated against known incidents, so the dashboard tells the same story as case notes. Weekly reviews create the operating rhythm—each red or amber trend leads to a specific decision: adjust a workflow, fix a data feed, tune thresholds, retrain a model, or modify an automation gate. Track action items so owners remain accountable. A recommendation adoption rate above seventy percent indicates utility and trust; below forty percent signals friction, poor relevance, or weak workflow integration.

System 5: Governance and Guardrails

Governance protects speed and trust when AI influences security actions. The core artifacts are decision logs (Chapter 8's structured logging applied here), DPIA one-pagers for models touching personal data, bias audit checklists with subgroup parity checks, and published human-review thresholds per safety tier. Vendor expectations for explainability, logs, and evidence support become delivery requirements, not optional extras. DPIA coverage at one hundred percent for relevant models sets a clear standard. Decision-log completeness above ninety-eight percent builds confidence for audits and incident reviews.

System 6: Continuous Improvement

Continuous improvement keeps models reliable through release discipline, drift monitoring, adversarial testing (Chapter 7), and resilience drills. Start with a model release checklist: evaluation sets, regression tests, drift baselines, rollback steps, approvals, and evidence storage. Schedule AI red-teaming on a cadence (Chapter 2). Run AI-off drills with objectives and success criteria—outages and vendor incidents happen, and teams need practice. Build a feedback-labeling loop for true positives, false positives, and misses, tied to evaluation and retraining rules. Feedback coverage above eighty percent gives a learning loop that improves; low coverage signals a program losing momentum.

Readiness Assessment: Where Are You Today?

Before launching or expanding an AI security program, score your organization against each of the six systems. The matrix below provides a simple 1–5 scale. The lowest-scoring system is your starting point—strengthening it first produces the highest marginal return.

Table 10.1: Readiness assessment matrix. Score each system 1–5. Your lowest score is your starting point.

System	1—Not started	2—Ad hoc	3—Defined	4—Measured	5—Optimized
Outcomes & Scope	No outcome statements, no use cases selected	Use cases chosen without baselines or owners	Outcomes documented, owners named, baselines captured	KPIs tracked weekly with action items from reviews	Scope expands based on proven performance; automation tiers tuned quarterly
Data Readiness	Log sources unknown or unmapped	Some feeds connected but no normalization or monitoring	Crown-jewel map exists; identifiers and timestamps aligned	Feed health monitored; broken-feed days tracked; data contracts in place	Coverage above 95%; schema drift auto detected; continuous validation

(Contd.)

System	1—Not started	2—Ad hoc	3—Defined	4—Measured	5—Optimized
Phased Deployment	AI running in production without shadow baseline	Shadow mode attempted but not measured	Shadow, assist, and auto tiers defined with rollback plans	Reversal rate tracked; tiers adjusted based on evidence	Automation scope expands methodically; reversal rate below 2%
Measurable Performance	No KPIs defined	Dashboards exist but not tied to decisions	KPI cards with owners; weekly reviews with action items	Trends drive workflow changes; adoption rate above 70%	Metrics tied to business outcomes; false positive and dwell time compound
Governance	No DPIAs; no decision logs; no bias audits	Some documentation exists but inconsistent	DPIAs complete; decision logs mandatory; bias audit on schedule	Evidence produced continuously via GRC agents (Ch 8)	Audit-ready at any time; governance embedded in daily operations
Continuous Improvement	No release discipline; no adversarial testing	Ad hoc retraining when issues surface	Release checklist enforced; red-team cadence scheduled	Drift monitored continuously; AI-off drills run quarterly	Feedback loop closes within a sprint; every incident improves detection

A practical use of this matrix: score each system, identify the lowest, and make that system the first-quarter focus. An organization at level 2 on Data Readiness and level 4 on everything else will see its AI program limited by data quality, not by model capability. Fixing the constraint produces the biggest improvement.

A 12-Month Plan Leaders Can Run

Quarter 1: Foundations. Baselines, shadow mode, and data health. Guardrails published. Assist mode introduced for correlation and IR summarization. Weekly reviews begin and stay consistent.

Quarter 2: Evidence and early automation. Low-risk automation enabled with tracked reversal rates. DPIAs completed for relevant models. First bias audit executed with remediation tracked. Time-saved metrics published.

Quarter 3: Expansion and adversarial testing. Identity and privilege cleanup added to scope. Adaptive access workflows introduced. Adversarial testing cadence begins and feeds into model releases. Coverage expands toward crown jewels.

Quarter 4: Scale and resilience. Automation scope widened to crown-jewel systems. Reversal rate held below two percent. AI-off drills run. Post-quantum readiness inventory added to leadership reporting (Chapter 9). Program demonstrates compound improvement across MTTD, MTTR, false positives, and root-cause clarity.

The Executive Dashboard That Fits on One Screen

A board-ready dashboard can fit into four tiles with target bands and clear triggers. Tile 1—Speed: MTTD, MTTR, MTTC with target improvements for AI-assisted domains. Tile 2—Quality: precision, recall, false positive trends, recommendation adoption rate. Tile 3—Coverage and Identity: crown-jewel coverage, high-risk logins blocked, privilege reduction progress. Tile 4—Governance: DPIA coverage, bias audits on schedule, decision-log completeness, automation reversal rate. Each tile has an owner and a trigger that drives action during weekly reviews. A chart without a decision pathway becomes background noise.

Two Sprints to Value in 30 Days

Sprint 1 (days 1–14). Run shadow email correlation for BEC and incident-response summary drafting for analyst review. Target: measurable triage time reduction and fewer duplicates reaching analysts. Capture baselines from real incidents.

Sprint 2 (days 15–30). Enable two low-blast-radius actions with clear approval and rollback—endpoint isolation for strong ransomware signals and step-up authentication for high-risk logins. Track reversal daily. Tune thresholds early. Publish first results to stakeholders.

Case Study: From Pilot to Policy in 90 Days

A composite enterprise starts with two outcomes: faster resolution for identity-led incidents and less analyst time wasted on duplicate alerts. Leadership wants proof inside one quarter, plus confidence that the program can handle audits and staffing changes.

The first month focuses on baselines, data health, and shadow mode. Two use cases are selected: BEC correlation and identity triage. Baselines are captured for MTTD, MTTR, and root-cause clarity. The data platform owner builds the crown-jewel map, aligns identifiers, and deploys feed monitoring. Shadow mode begins with analysts labeling outcomes as part of the normal workflow.

The second month moves into assisted workflows and evidence discipline. AI drafts incident summaries and suggests next steps; analysts choose actions and record feedback. Weekly reviews begin. Models touching personal data receive DPIAs. Decision logs become mandatory. A bias and quality review records findings and schedules the next review date.

The third month enables two low-risk automations: endpoint isolation for strong ransomware signals and step-up authentication for high-risk logins. Reversal stays under two percent through threshold tuning. The executive dashboard goes live with four tiles. Leadership sees fewer duplicates per analyst, fewer minutes per case, faster containment, higher root-cause clarity, and decision logs that support audit checks without scrambling. The quarter ends with a repeatable rhythm: weekly ops reviews, quarterly adversarial tests, a release checklist, and scheduled AI-off drills. The program earns trust because safety tiers and reversal tracking protect business continuity while measurable outcomes show real improvement.

Executive Takeaways

- **Operating-model maturity must match tooling maturity.** Tools improve outcomes only when program mechanics—baselines, owners, data health, governance—stay strong.
- **Start with two high-impact use cases, instrumented from day one.** Early scope determines whether the program earns trust. BEC correlation and identity triage are reliable starting points.
- **Automate low-blast-radius actions first.** Track reversal rate. Tune thresholds early. Protect trust and business continuity before expanding the scope.
- **Treat decision logs as a product capability.** Evidence unlocks audit readiness, learning, and defensibility—Chapter 8's structured logging applied operationally.
- **Run a standing cadence for adversarial tests, bias audits, model reviews, and AI-off drills.** Reliability stays stable through pressure when the cadence is protected.
- **Use the readiness matrix to find the constraint.** The lowest-scoring system is the starting point. Fixing the constraint produces the biggest improvement.
- **Scale when baselines, outcomes, and governance sit inside green bands.** Growth follows proof, not optimism.

- **The program compounds when every incident improves future prevention.** The closed loop from Chapter 5 is the mechanism; the operating model is the discipline that keeps it running.

End-of-Chapter Reflection Questions

- Score your organization against each of the six systems in Table 10.1. Which system scored lowest, and what would the first-quarter plan to raise it by one level look like?
- For your current AI security program, can you name the owner of each outcome statement? If ownership is unclear, what decision would clarify it this week?
- When was the last time a red trend on your security dashboard led to a specific, tracked action item with a named owner and a deadline? If the answer is "never" or "I don't remember," what does that say about the weekly review cadence?
- For every automated security action in production, is the reversal rate tracked? What is the current number, and who reviews it?
- If your AI vendor changed models, raised prices, or experienced an outage tomorrow, how quickly could your program continue operating? What is the rollback plan?
- How many days would it take your program to produce a complete audit evidence package for every AI system influencing security decisions? If the answer is more than two, what is missing?
- Which of the two 30-day sprint use cases—BEC correlation or ransomware isolation—would produce the most visible value in your environment? What would you need to start next Monday?
- Does every incident your SOC handles today feed back into a specific improvement—a new detection rule, a tightened pipeline gate, an updated threat model? If not, where does the feedback loop break?

Conclusion

SECURITY WITH AI THAT HOLDS UP IN REAL CONDITIONS

This book began with a race—attackers scaling operations while defenders pushed for speed in detection, decision-making, and containment. Ten chapters later, the race has not ended. It has sharpened. Adversaries use AI to craft better lures, evade smarter defenses, and probe systems at machine speed. Defenders use AI to correlate signals across six surfaces, respond in minutes rather than days, and close the loop between production incidents and upstream prevention. The edge belongs to the team that compounds learning faster.

What Holds Up

Several themes have persisted across every chapter, and they hold up because they are structural, not situational.

Fundamentals decide whether AI produces clarity or noise. Patching, identity discipline, segmentation, tested backups, asset inventory, and consistent telemetry are the substrate AI runs on. Organizations that invested in baseline hardening before scaling AI detection reported fewer false positives, faster analyst adoption, and measurable drops in response time. Organizations that skipped that phase reported the opposite. AI amplifies whatever is already there—good fundamentals become great outcomes; weak fundamentals become louder alerts.

The SSDLC and the SOC are two halves of a single learning system. Chapter 4's AI-powered SSDLC and Chapter 5's AI-powered SOC create a closed loop where development insights improve detection, and incident learnings improve prevention. Organizations that instrument this loop explicitly—with tickets, metrics, and ownership for each feedback path—improve measurably faster than organizations that leave it informal.

Human-in-the-loop placement is a design decision with business consequences. Destructive actions need human approval. Reversible actions can run with supervision. High-confidence, low-blast-radius actions can be fully automated with a kill switch. Documenting these boundaries, reviewing them quarterly, and expanding automation scope as reliability is demonstrated is the operating discipline that prevents both over-automation and bottleneck-induced paralysis.

Governance is product work, not paperwork. The EU AI Act, DPDPA, NIST AI RMF, ISO 42001, and sector regulations together make evidence a daily deliverable. GRC agents that pull evidence from live systems, sub-processor due diligence that runs before data moves, and structured decision logging that supports the user, the auditor, and the tuning team simultaneously—these are what "governance as a product" looks like in practice.

AI systems are assets that need securing, not just tools that provide security. Prompt injection, model poisoning, training-data extraction, agent overreach, and supply-chain compromise are real attack categories with real incidents. Programs that treat AI only as a defender miss half the picture. Inventory, access controls, prompt and output safety, agent governance, and red-teaming cadence are the control set.

The Path from Interest to Capability

Chapter 10's six-system operating model provides the practical path. Start with two high-impact use cases instrumented from day one. Capture baselines so progress is visible. Phase deployment through shadow, assist, and automation tiers with reversal tracking. Measure what matters and review it weekly with owners who can act. Govern with evidence produced continuously, not assembled under pressure. Improve through release discipline, adversarial testing, and feedback loops that close within a sprint.

The readiness assessment matrix tells you where to start. Score each system. Find the constraint. Fix it first. Then expand.

A Final Thought

Security rewards preparedness, learning speed, and operating discipline under pressure. Tools will evolve. Adversaries will adapt. The environment will expand into new places—quantum-era cryptography, sovereign AI infrastructure, edge devices in factories and fleets, and AI agents with broader autonomy. Organizations that keep fundamentals strong, invest in people and adaptable systems, treat governance as a daily discipline, and compound learning from every incident will handle shocks better and earn trust when it matters most.

Technology is a precondition. The operating discipline is the differentiator. And the closed loop—where every incident makes the next one less likely, every finding sharpens the next detection, and every quarter's measurement informs the next quarter's investment—is where programs that hold up are built.

ANNEXURES

AI-Driven Security in Practice

The following annexures complement the strategic themes explored throughout this book by illustrating how three leading security platforms are integrating AI to improve security posture across distinct domains. Each annexure is presented independently, covering a different category of the modern security stack: cloud security, offensive and application security testing, and application security posture management.

Annexure A

AI-DRIVEN CLOUD DEFENSE IN PRACTICE

Applying Runtime-First CNAPP with Upwind

Bridging Strategy and Execution in Modern Cloud Security

This annexure complements the themes explored in Fortified by AI, translating strategic principles into a practical, cloud-native security implementation using a modern Cloud-Native Application Protection Platform (CNAPP).

1. From AI Strategy to Cloud Reality

One of the core arguments of Fortified by AI is that AI delivers defensive value only when grounded in real operational context. Static analysis, snapshot-based posture checks, and disconnected security tools fail in environments where workloads are ephemeral, APIs are dynamic, and identities change continuously.

This challenge is most visible in cloud environments. Traditional cloud security posture management (CSPM) tools focus on configuration correctness but struggle to answer a more critical question: Which risks actually matter in production right now?

Industry analysis and investor research highlight a market shift toward runtime-first cloud security, where live execution context determines priority, not theoretical exposure. Upwind positions its Cloud-Native Application Protection Platform (CNAPP) around this exact principle—starting security analysis inside running workloads, rather than outside them.

2. Understanding the Upwind CNAPP Architecture

Upwind's CNAPP is designed around an inside-out security model, which differs materially from legacy CNAPP platforms that rely primarily on static configuration scans.

According to Upwind's platform documentation and third-party analysis, the system deploys lightweight runtime sensors that observe process behavior, network traffic, API calls, and container and workload execution paths.

These runtime signals are continuously streamed and enriched with cloud metadata, identity context, and service relationships to construct a real execution graph of the environment.

This aligns directly with the book's position (reinforced in Chapter 5's AI-SOC telemetry and Chapter 10's data readiness system) that AI systems must be fed high-fidelity, real-world signals to avoid producing noise, bias, or false confidence.

3. AI Embedded in the Upwind Platform: Beyond Marketing Claims

Upwind does not position AI as a generic "black box" decision maker. Instead, AI is embedded in correlation, prioritization, and posture evaluation layers of the platform.

Public disclosures and product announcements indicate that Upwind's AI capabilities are used to correlate runtime signals with configuration data, determine whether vulnerabilities are actually reachable in production, and prioritize findings based on real execution paths, not static severity scores.

This approach reduces alert fatigue by focusing on exploitable conditions rather than dormant weaknesses, a challenge widely acknowledged in CNAPP and CSPM markets—the same reachability-first principle that Fortified by AI applies to SAST and SCA in Chapter 4 and to SOC alert triage in Chapter 5.

4. Defending Against Cloud Configuration Risks with Runtime Context

Traditional CSPM tools flag misconfigurations equally, regardless of whether the affected resource is exposed, active, or reachable. Upwind's runtime-powered CSPM enhancements address this gap by incorporating live production behavior into posture management decisions.

According to industry coverage, Upwind's CNAPP introduces posture rules that rank misconfigurations based on actual runtime exposure, allow security teams to define custom posture frameworks using live data, and provide executive-level posture dashboards grounded in real risk.

This enables continuous improvement of cloud security posture by ensuring teams fix what matters most first, rather than chasing compliance noise.

5. Runtime Sensors for Vulnerability and Threat Detection

A recurring theme in Fortified by AI is the importance of reachability analysis. Upwind's runtime sensors support this by observing which services communicate with each other, which vulnerabilities sit on active execution paths, and whether an exposed component is reachable through APIs, identities, or data flows.

Investor research highlights that this capability allows security teams to distinguish between vulnerabilities in dormant services and vulnerabilities that form part of a viable attack path.

This distinction is critical for modern cloud defense, where thousands of theoretical findings may exist, but only a small subset poses immediate risk.

6. AI Security and Agentic Workloads

As enterprises increasingly deploy AI services, models, and autonomous agents, the cloud attack surface expands beyond traditional compute and storage.

Upwind announced the integration of AI-native security capabilities directly into its CNAPP, extending runtime visibility into AI models and inference endpoints, agent behavior and decision chains, and data flows between AI services and cloud resources.

These capabilities—described as inside-out AI security—apply the same runtime-first philosophy to AI workloads, enabling security teams to observe how AI systems behave in production rather than relying on static assumptions.

This directly supports the book's guidance in Chapter 6 that AI systems must themselves be observable, governable, and accountable—treated as assets that need securing, not just tools that provide security.

7. Continuous Improvement of Cloud Security Posture

A key leadership takeaway from Fortified by AI is that security posture is not a fixed state—it is a continuously evolving system.

Upwind's CNAPP supports this model by continuously ingesting runtime telemetry, updating posture and risk prioritization dynamically, and enabling feedback loops between detection, remediation, and policy refinement.

By grounding posture management in real execution data, organizations can move from periodic audits to continuous posture improvement, a model increasingly favored by regulators and industry frameworks—and central to the 6-System Operating Model presented in Chapter 10.

8. Strategic Fit for Security Leaders

For CISOs and cloud security leaders, the relevance of Upwind's approach lies not in tool consolidation alone, but in operational alignment with AI-driven defense principles: evidence over assumption, runtime context over static snapshots, prioritization over volume, and human-guided decision making supported by AI.

These principles echo the core thesis of Fortified by AI and demonstrate how AI-driven cyber defense can be operationalized in cloud-native environments.

9. Learn More and Engage

Organizations interested in exploring runtime-first CNAPP and AI-driven cloud security can find additional information, documentation, and contact options via Upwind's official website: upwind.io

Closing Perspective

This annexure illustrates how the strategic concepts outlined in Fortified by AI translate into real-world cloud security practice. By embedding AI within runtime intelligence, posture management, and continuous feedback loops, platforms such as Upwind demonstrate how AI can augment—not replace—human security leadership.

In an era defined by ephemeral infrastructure and autonomous systems, runtime-first, AI-assisted defense is no longer optional—it is foundational.

Annexure B

AI-DRIVEN OFFENSIVE SECURITY IN PRACTICE

Applying Continuous, AI-Assisted Pentesting with Astra Security

Bridging Strategy and Execution in Modern Application Security

This annexure complements the themes explored in Fortified by AI, translating strategic principles into a practical, offensive-security implementation using a modern, AI-assisted penetration testing and application security platform.

1. From AI Strategy to Offensive Security Reality

One of the core arguments of Fortified by AI is that AI delivers defensive value only when grounded in real attacker behavior and operational context. Static assessments, point-in-time pentests, and checklist-driven scans fail to reflect how modern attackers operate—continuously, creatively, and at scale.

This challenge is most visible in application and API security. Traditional penetration testing often answers a limited question: Was the application secure at the time of testing? What does not consistently answer is: How does security posture evolve as code, dependencies, APIs, and business logic change?

Industry practice increasingly favors continuous, AI-assisted offensive testing, where live environments are evaluated repeatedly using attacker-style techniques rather than periodic snapshots. Astra Security positions its platform around this principle by combining automated DAST, expert-led pen testing, and an in-house Attack AI engine into a single, continuous workflow.

2. Understanding the Astra Security Platform Architecture

Astra Security's platform is designed as a hybrid offensive security system, blending automation with human expertise. Rather than replacing penetration testers, the platform augments them.

At a high level, the architecture brings together automated DAST scanning across web applications, APIs, and cloud assets; AI-assisted test case generation derived from real-world pen testing knowledge; manual validation and exploitation by security experts; and centralized vulnerability management and collaboration workflows.

This hybrid model aligns with the book's position in Chapter 1 that AI is most effective when paired with human judgment through the HITL (human-in-the-loop) framework, particularly in adversarial domains like security testing.

Beyond application and API security, Astra's platform extends to cloud security posture management (scanning cloud infrastructure for misconfigurations, exposed assets, and compliance gaps), ensuring that AI-assisted offensive testing covers the full attack surface across the six surfaces introduced in Chapter 1—not just application layers.

3. AI Embedded in Astra: Beyond Automation

Astra does not present AI as a generic scanner. Instead, AI is embedded as an offensive intelligence layer that supports scale, consistency, and learning.

Public platform descriptions indicate that Astra's AI capabilities are used to generate and evolve attack test cases based on real pentest findings, continuously scan applications using attacker-style logic rather than static rules, and assist engineers with contextual remediation guidance during vulnerability resolution.

Critically, Astra's findings are validated before delivery, combining automated detection with expert review to ensure zero false positives in reported vulnerabilities. Security and engineering teams act on confirmed issues, instead of just noise.

This approach reflects a key theme from Fortified by AI: AI should amplify expert workflows, not attempt to fully automate adversarial reasoning.

4. AI-Assisted Pentesting and Red-Team-Style Thinking

A recurring theme in Fortified by AI is the need to think like an attacker—without losing governance and control. Chapter 7 maps adversarial AI risk across three layers, including attackers weaponizing AI to scale classic tactics. Astra's platform applies AI to support red-team-style exploration at scale, while maintaining structured oversight.

AI supports identifying combinations of weaknesses that may form exploit chains, expanding coverage across large application and API surfaces, and supporting expert testers in focusing on higher-order logic and abuse cases.

This reflects an important balance: AI increases breadth and speed, while human pentesters retain responsibility for interpretation, exploitation, validation, and reporting.

As AI-driven applications and LLM integrations become primary attack targets, Astra's platform includes dedicated LLM security testing—evaluating prompt injection, model manipulation, and data leakage risks specific to AI-powered product surfaces. This directly connects to the OWASP Top 10 for LLM introduced in Chapter 2 and the prompt injection attack taxonomy in Chapter 7.

5. Trust Platform and Verifiable Security Posture

Beyond detection, Astra's Trust Platform focuses on communicating security posture to external stakeholders. Instead of static reports, organizations can present consolidated, up-to-date evidence of security testing activities, certifications, and remediation progress.

This supports the book's governance-as-product principle from Chapter 8: security must be demonstrable, not assumed. Transparency becomes part of the defensive strategy, particularly in vendor risk management and compliance-driven environments where the sub-processor due diligence framework from Chapter 8 applies.

6. CREST-Aligned and Expert-Led Testing

For organizations requiring formal assurance, Astra offers penetration testing services aligned with recognized industry standards and methodologies, including CREST-aligned practices.

This ensures that while AI accelerates testing and coverage, human-led assessment remains central for high-assurance use cases such as regulatory reviews, customer assurance, and risk acceptance.

7. Continuous Improvement of Application Security Posture

A key leadership takeaway from Fortified by AI is that security posture is never static. Astra's platform supports this model by enabling continuous discovery of new vulnerabilities as applications evolve, revalidation of fixes and mitigations, and ongoing collaboration between security and engineering teams.

By embedding offensive testing into everyday workflows, organizations move closer to the living security posture described in the book's closed-loop SSDLC-SOC model (Chapter 5, Figure 5.1), where every finding sharpens future prevention.

8. *Strategic Fit for Security Leaders*

For CISOs and application security leaders, Astra's relevance lies in its alignment with AI-driven defense principles: attacker-centric testing over checklist compliance, continuous validation over annual exercises, AI-assisted scale with human accountability, and evidence-based trust rather than static assurance.

These principles directly echo the core thesis of Fortified by AI and demonstrate how AI-driven cyber defense can be operationalized in offensive security programs.

Astra Security's platform recorded 6.8 million vulnerabilities across 150,000+ scans and 8,000+ pentest engagements in 2025, covering web, API, cloud, mobile, and network infrastructure across 400+ organizations worldwide.

Closing Perspective

This annexure illustrates how the strategic concepts outlined in Fortified by AI translate into modern penetration testing and application security practice. By embedding AI into continuous offensive testing, expert-led validation, and transparent trust reporting, platforms such as Astra Security demonstrate how AI can strengthen—not replace—human-led security programs.

In an era of rapid development, API-driven architectures, and AI-assisted attackers, continuous, AI-augmented pentesting is no longer optional—it is foundational.

Annexure C

AI-DRIVEN APPLICATION SECURITY POSTURE MANAGEMENT IN PRACTICE

Applying Active ASPM with OX Security

Bridging Strategy and Execution in Modern Application Security Posture

This annexure complements the themes explored in Fortified by AI, translating strategic principles into a practical, application security posture management implementation using a modern, AI-powered Active ASPM platform.

1. From AI Strategy to Application Security Posture Reality

One of the core arguments of Fortified by AI is that AI delivers defensive value only when grounded in real operational context. Fragmented scanners, disconnected dashboards, and siloed findings fail to provide the unified view that security leaders need to make sound prioritization decisions.

This challenge is most visible in application security. Organizations deploy multiple tools—SAST, DAST, SCA, IaC scanners, secrets detection, container security—each producing its own findings, its own severity scores, and its own alert stream. The result is tool sprawl, inconsistent data, excessive alerts, and wasted time as security teams struggle to create a coherent strategy from disconnected signals.

Industry analysis and analyst research, including Gartner's recognition of the ASPM category, highlight a market shift toward unified, posture-driven application security that correlates findings across the full software development lifecycle. OX Security positions its Active ASPM platform around this exact principle—unifying application security practices with comprehensive visibility, contextual prioritization, and automated response from code to cloud.

2. Understanding the OX Security Platform Architecture

OX Security's Active ASPM platform is designed as a unified, code-first security system that embeds detection and response across the entire software development lifecycle. Rather than aggregating scanner output passively, the platform actively correlates, contextualizes, and prioritizes findings.

At a high level, the architecture brings together ten native scanning tools that serve as an AppSec Data Fabric, covering SAST, SCA, secrets detection, IaC scanning, SBOM generation, API discovery, and container security. These native capabilities integrate seamlessly with over one hundred third-party technologies, offering unmatched flexibility in how organizations ingest and normalize security data across their existing tool chain.

The platform's proprietary Pipeline Bill of Materials (PBOM) technology provides end-to-end mapping from code repositories to cloud workloads, capturing every artifact in the software supply chain. This aligns directly with the AI-enhanced SSDLC model in Chapter 4, where security must cover the full lifecycle—plan, build, test, deploy, run, and observe—with visibility that no single scanner can provide alone.

3. AI Embedded in OX Security: Beyond Aggregation

OX Security does not present AI as a generic alert aggregator. Instead, AI is embedded as a contextual intelligence layer that transforms how findings are understood, prioritized, and acted upon.

The platform's Code Projection technology maps runtime behavior back to its originating source code, providing actionable insights into reachable, exploitable vulnerabilities. This capability directly supports the reachability analysis theme from Chapter 4—the recognition that a vulnerability in an imported library only matters if the vulnerable function is actually called in a production execution path.

OX's Active Context Analysis uses a three-layer model to evaluate threats beyond surface-level severity scores, incorporating environmental context, business impact, and threat intelligence. The platform enriches findings with trusted sources, including CVSS, CISA KEV, and EPSS, to produce defensible, evidence-backed prioritization. According to OX Security, this approach reduces false positives by up to 97%, ensuring teams focus on the critical subset of issues that pose real-world risk rather than drowning in noise.

This approach reflects a key theme from Fortified by AI: AI should reduce the cognitive load on security teams by surfacing signals over volume, enabling faster, higher-quality decisions.

4. Securing the Software Supply Chain with PBOM and OSC&R

A recurring theme in Fortified by AI is the importance of software supply chain security—from the CI/CD pipeline security framework in Chapter 4 to the model and data supply-chain integrity controls in Chapter 6. OX Security addresses this through its Pipeline Bill of Materials (PBOM) technology, which provides comprehensive visibility into every component, dependency, and artifact in the development pipeline—from source control through CI/CD to production deployment.

As a founding member of the Open Software Supply Chain Attack Reference (OSC&R) framework, OX contributes to the industry's shared understanding of supply chain attack patterns and defensive practices. The platform's attack path analysis enables users to visualize and quickly address security concerns from a single screen, mapping how a vulnerability in a dependency, a misconfiguration in a pipeline, or a secret exposed in a container connects to a viable attack path.

This capability directly supports the book's guidance that treating the CI/CD pipeline as critical infrastructure requires visibility into the full supply chain, not just the application code.

5. AI-Assisted Remediation and Developer Collaboration

Finding vulnerabilities is half the work. Fixing them is the other half, and the place where many security programs lose their engineering partners. OX Security addresses this through automated, no-code workflow-driven remediation that eliminates manual handoffs.

The platform can block risky merges automatically, open tickets with full context, generate audit-ready reports for compliance frameworks, and route findings to the right team with the right priority. Security policies can be defined once and applied consistently across repositories, pipelines, and environments.

This aligns with the book's emphasis on AI-led remediation that moves beyond "here is a defect" to "here is the specific fix, with context, routed to the right person, with evidence." The HITL tiering framework from Chapter 1—fully automated for mechanical fixes, human-on-the-loop for routine fixes, human-in-the-loop for security-critical code—maps directly to how OX's workflow automation can be configured.

6. VibeSec™: Active Runtime Protection

OX Security's VibeSec™ framework represents the platform's evolution from passive posture monitoring to active runtime protection. VibeSec uses AI-driven context to detect policy violations in real time and enforce corrective actions across the SDLC.

As organizations increasingly deploy AI-generated code through agentic development tools—Cursor, Claude Code, GitHub Copilot, and autonomous agents, as explored in Chapter 4—VibeSec provides a mechanism to automatically prevent vulnerabilities in AI-generated code, ensuring security from the first line. This active approach keeps protection aligned with development speed, so teams can ship software faster without compromising safety.

The OX AI Data Lake, a continuously updated repository of security intelligence, combines global threat signals with organization-specific context covering code, APIs, cloud, and runtime. This ensures posture decisions are accurate, current, and grounded in the organization's actual risk profile rather than generic severity scores.

7. Compliance and Regulatory Alignment

A key leadership concern addressed throughout Fortified by AI is the need for security evidence that satisfies regulatory and compliance requirements. Chapter 8's comprehensive regulatory landscape—covering the EU AI Act, GDPR, India's DPDPA, ISO 42001, NIST AI RMF, and sector-specific rules—makes clear that governance must be continuous, not periodic.

OX Security's Active ASPM platform helps organizations maintain pace with the evolving regulatory environment by providing a software lineage list aligned with standards such as the EU Cybersecurity Act, CISA guidance, and the NIST Cybersecurity Framework. The platform generates audit-ready reports and maintains continuous compliance evidence as a by-product of daily operations—supporting the book's governance-as-product principle, where evidence is produced automatically by GRC agents rather than assembled under audit pressure.

8. Strategic Fit for Security Leaders

For CISOs and application security leaders, OX Security's relevance lies in its alignment with AI-driven defense principles: unified posture over fragmented tooling, contextual prioritization over raw severity scores, code-to-cloud visibility over point-in-time snapshots, and automated remediation with developer-first workflow integration.

These principles directly echo the core thesis of Fortified by AI and demonstrate how AI-driven cyber defense can be operationalized in application security posture management programs.

Recognized as a Gartner Cool Vendor and a SINET 16 Innovator, OX Security is trusted by global enterprises and technology-forward companies. Founded by industry leaders Neatsun Ziv, former VP of Check Point's Cyber Security business unit, and Lior Arzi from Check

Point's Security Division, OX's Active ASPM platform empowers organizations to take the first step toward eliminating manual AppSec practices while enabling scalable, secure development.

9. Learn More and Engage

Organizations interested in exploring Active ASPM and AI-driven application security posture management can find additional information, documentation, and contact options via OX Security's official website: **https://www.ox.security/**

Closing Perspective

This annexure illustrates how the strategic concepts outlined in Fortified by AI translate into modern application security posture management practice. By unifying AppSec tools into a single adaptive system, embedding AI into contextual prioritization and remediation, and providing code-to-cloud visibility across the software supply chain, platforms such as OX Security demonstrate how AI can transform—not merely supplement—application security programs.

In an era of AI-accelerated development, complex software supply chains, and regulatory pressure that demands continuous evidence, Active ASPM is no longer optional—it is foundational.

ABOUT THE AUTHOR

Parvesh Ahlawat is a cybersecurity leader, strategist, and practitioner with over two decades of experience protecting enterprise systems across some of the most demanding environments in technology, defense, and regulated industry.

His career began in the Indian Air Force, where he served in a role that combined technology operations with the discipline, precision, and mission-critical thinking that military service demands. The Air Force taught him something that no certification or vendor training ever could: when systems fail under pressure, it is not the technology that holds the line—it is the people, the process, and the operating discipline behind it. That lesson became the foundation for everything that followed, and it runs through every chapter of this book. The rigor of military operations—clear accountability, rehearsed procedures, decision-making under uncertainty, and the habit of preparing for the scenario you hope never arrives—shaped the way he approaches cybersecurity leadership to this day.

After his service, Parvesh moved into the technology industry, where he built a career spanning application security, cloud security, security operations, secure software development, identity and access management, and enterprise risk governance. He has designed and led security programs for organizations ranging from high-growth startups to global enterprises, across sectors including financial services, legal technology, SaaS, healthcare technology, and critical infrastructure. His work has consistently sat at the intersection of engineering and leadership—building security architectures that scale, standing up SOC and incident response capabilities, embedding security into CI/CD pipelines and DevSecOps workflows, and advising boards and CXO stakeholders on risk posture, cyber resilience, and strategic investment.

He has built scalable security frameworks that align with business priorities rather than fighting against them. He has led threat modeling programs, secure development practices, and detection engineering initiatives across complex multi-cloud and hybrid environments. He has recruited, mentored, and led high-performing security teams with a strong emphasis on accountability, continuous learning, and the kind of operational discipline that holds up during real incidents—not just during planning sessions.

In recent years, his focus has shifted to the intersection of artificial intelligence and cybersecurity—the space this book occupies. He has led the adoption of AI-driven detection and response, governed the deployment of agentic AI tools within engineering teams, navigated the regulatory landscape across multiple jurisdictions, including GDPR, India's DPDPA, and the EU AI Act, and built governance frameworks for AI systems that influence security decisions. His perspective is grounded in the reality of production—where models drift, adversaries adapt, false positives erode trust, and governance is not a slide deck but a set of evidence that a regulator, a customer, or an internal reviewer can examine at any time.

Parvesh holds an MTech from BITS Pilani and an MCA from The ICFAI University, Tripura. He is based in Ahmedabad, India.

Why This Book Exists

This book exists because the questions Parvesh faced daily as a security leader—how to trust an AI recommendation at 3 AM, how to govern agentic coding tools without blocking engineering velocity, how to comply with DPDPA and GDPR and the EU AI Act with the same team, how to explain to a board that AI is both the solution and a new attack surface—did not have a single, practical reference that answered them in the language of someone who has to make it work in production.

Every framework, case study, and reflection question in this book comes from the work itself—the incidents responded to, the programs built and rebuilt, the governance frameworks that held under audit and the ones that did not, the teams led through difficult moments, and the lessons those moments produced. The Indian Air Force taught him to prepare for the scenario he hoped would never arrive. Two decades in cybersecurity taught him that it always does. This book is the preparation he wishes he had been handed earlier.

www.ingramcontent.com/pod-product-compliance
Lightning Source LLC
LaVergne TN
LVHW060038210926
848481LV00013B/3894